The Heat's On, Baby!

(A Book for Chile Heads)

By Carol Lazzeri-Casey

The "SAVOUR THE FLAVOUR" Series

BookSurge, LLC
North Charleston, SC

To order additional copies:
visit www.savour-flavour.com
or call 866.308.6235, Ext. 120

Savour the Flavour
8 chilies!
Carol

Edited by Gail Ellen King

ISBN: 1-4196-1150-X

Printed in the United States of America
North Charleston, South Carolina

A warm and sincere thank you

to those courageous men and women

who have fearlessly sampled and critiqued the recipes contained in this book.

To my very dear friends

- Ivan and Nola -

who instilled in their five children their personal recipe for life…

"If you try your best in every endeavor, you need never look back."

To them, I dedicate The Heat's On, Baby!

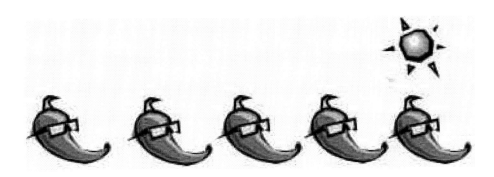

Contents

I *LOVE* CHILES! I love their endearing warmth, their enchantment and mystique…their legend and lore. Vivid colours of rich red, mahogony with crimson hues, canary yellow, glorious orange, crispy green. I love savouring the flavours of succulent fruit, hints of cocoa and smoky, earthy undertones. *I love their heat! ... their lip smacking, eye popping appeal! ... that relentless slap-in-the-face, knock-you-out, and leave-you-for-dead bolt of lightening!*

So, okay, **YES**, I relent - I am, unquestionably, without a doubt…a Chile Head! And I am admitting it *proudly*!

For a moment, though, let's put aside the craziness of it all and look at what might be considered the "practical" side of consuming chiles…

First justification…chiles are full of Vitamin C! And *red* chiles are loaded with beta carotene. In addition, the nutritional aspect of hot peppers that gives them their burn (capsaicin) is beginning to show signs of having a positive effect on blood cholesterol as well as contributing as an anticoagulant. Oh, and don't forget: chiles are great for your metabolism because spicy foods help you burn more calories. So…let's not discount *these* tidbits of information as we analyze why we love the pain; and, incidentally, *speaking of pain*, chiles can also be used as pain *relievers*! Yes, *believe it or not!* In fact, there are various pain-relieving products on the market that *contain* capsaicin. And they are making their unprecedented claim to fame!

And if *that's* not enough, some Chile Heads have claimed to experience a "high" from eating spicy, fiery foods. Theory says when you experience a chile "burn", the brain releases endorphins creating a very pleasant, intoxicating sensation throughout your body. Though you may fear not, mis amigos! The euphoric experience is *perfectly safe!* (*I've yet to hear of an arrest for driving under the influence of chile peppers!*)

Also, of course (on the far side), you can always try using chiles *to rid yourself and others of bad luck, for casting spells, and other forms of bewitchery!…not to mention burning them to rid your home of werewolves!* So, given all of *this* enlightening information, why *wouldn't* we totally appreciate the full magical potential of these fiery little fruits!

…Alas, yes, some do *still* believe eating chiles is justifiable reason for institutionalization! (After all, let's face it…they *can* pack one *hell of a wallop!*) These naysayers seem to think heat and spice mask the flavour of foods and that anyone having such a "culinary idiosyncrasy" is a misfit in the finer world of gastronomical experiences. Well, if you too are a Chile Head, rest assured - because you are not alone and (*more than likely*) not insane! On the contrary, you can consider yourself someone who appreciates that the right combination and amount of chiles will actually make your taste buds *sing with delight* and intensify the appreciation of foods you eat!

So…to any disbeliever … WATCH OUT !!! We the Chile Heads of the world are coming with a POWERFUL punch … and we are **HOT**, **HOT**, **HOT**!

The Heat's On, Baby! So let's get going!!!

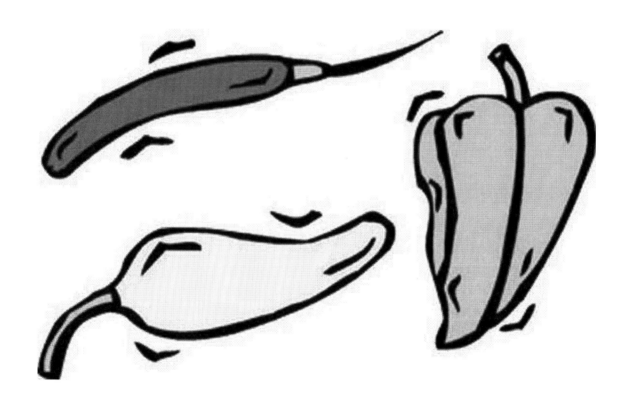

Hot Information

- *First…The (Confusing) Spelling*

- *Chilies…Not just "Tex-Mex"*

- *Types of Chilies*

- *Benefits of Eating Chilies*

- *Capsaicin Tolerance and "Addiction"*

- *A Word of Caution: CALIENTE! (HOT!)*

- *Availability of Chilies*

- *Selecting Chilies*

- *How to Store, Prepare, and Peel Fresh Chilies*

- *Using Dried Chilies*

- *Chile Powder Versus Chili Powder*

First…The (Confusing) Spelling

Are you (justifiably) wondering…what is it…chile or chili? The spelling can be somewhat confusing. But, simply put, the spelling "chile" refers to the hot chile pepper.   The spelling "chili" refers to the traditional Texas stew and, of course, "Chile" (with a capital "C") refers to the country in South America!

Chilies…Not Just "Tex-Mex"!

Although the use of chile peppers is thought to be synonymous with Mexican and Southwestern cuisine, chilies are actually an extremely popular ingredient worldwide. And, to prove that…I have included a few Italian, Japanese, Chinese dishes as well as some traditional dishes from Spain. Oh! And of course the infamous American cheese burger…served up with pepper Jack cheese and fresh mushrooms with a touch of hot sauce!

Yes…chilies *are* for everyone! But, the type of chile and its level of heat are *NOT!* So, let's take a look at the various…

Types of Chilies

Chile peppers are cultivated in a wide range of sizes, shapes, colours, flavours, and degrees of heat – from mellow to positively explosive! And why would we want to subject ourselves to such tortuous temptation? Because we are enlivened by the flavours and our senses are opened up to tantalizing, titillating, new adventures in eclectic eating!

There are reportedly over 60 varieties of chile peppers, nearly all of them belonging to the species capsaicin (pronounced kap-SAY-iss-sin).

Even though the following list is meant to help you distinguish a few of the more common chile pepper varieties, it can be tricky (if not altogether impossible) to determine *how* hot a pepper will be! Usually…the larger the chile pepper, the milder it is. But chilies of *any* variety can be inconsistent, varying widely in their bite.

The hot component in chile peppers comes from the capsaicin oil produced in the interior seedpod and veins (also referred to as ribs or membranes) of the chile. (The seeds only become pungent through their direct contact with the capsaicin.)

Capsaicin content *(or what I reverently call "pepper power"!)* is measured in several ways. The national standard is measurement through Scoville Heat Units; the other (more accurate but less widely used) is High Performance Liquid Chromatography (HPLC).

In 1912, a chemist by the name of Wilbur Scoville developed a method to measure the heat level of chilies in parts per million. He blended various ground chilies with a sugar and water solution. Individual taste testers then sipped the liquid in increasingly diluted concentration until the heat was no longer evident. This measurement of millions of drops of sugar and water solution was then translated into Scoville Heat Units in multiples of 100.   Since individual palates and response to the fire in chilies vary dramatically, this test has been questioned as to its accuracy. It does, however, enable categorization of the various types of chilies into different (albeit sometimes wide-ranging) heat levels.

The most accurate method for measuring chile heat is HPLC, whereby chilies are dried and ground. Their capsaicin is extracted and placed into a device for analysis and measurement. This more sophisticated—*and much more costly*—method of measurement is less widely used than the Scoville method.

But, despite any elaborate testing method, even chile peppers of the same type have *varying degrees of heat!* I've found that *sampling peppers before adding them to foods ensures optimal flavour adjustment*. At the very least, I recommend adding a small amount at a time while preparing your dish until the food reaches the desired degree of heat.

And, generally (but not always) the more mature the pepper, the hotter it will be. For instance, a red cherry or Anaheim can pack more punch than those that are green. Even soil, climate, and other conditions affect the amount of capsaicin in a pepper – not to mention peppers on the same plant differing to some degree! So, as you can see, each pepper has its own personality; therefore, the type of pepper you choose and the quantity you use should be highly discretionary!

The following is an *approximate* heat chart – "approximate" because, remember…depending on when the test was done, how immune the individual palates, etcetera, etcetera…you may find this does not absolutely mirror the peppers you select. So *(please)* take it at face value … and simply use it as a ***guide***!

Scoville Chart	
The Pepper	**Approximate Scoville Units**
Habañero	350,000-550,000
Scotch Bonnet	200,000-300,000
Chiltepin	60,000-100,000
Thai	70,000-80,000
Rocoto	50,000-100,000
Cayenne	30,000-50,000
Serrano	10,000-25,000
Jalapeño/Chipotle	3,500-8,000
Fresno	5,000
Casabel	3,000-5,000
Guero	2,500-5,000
Hungarian Wax	2,500-5,000
Ancho/Poblano	2,500-3,000
Chilaca/Pasilla	2,500
Cherry	100-3,500
Anaheim	1,000-1,500
New Mexico	500-1,000
Pimento	500
Paprika	100-500
Bell	0

Anaheim: Anaheim peppers are the most commonly used chilies in the United States. They carry a heat range from mild to moderately hot; but Anaheim peppers grown in California are generally much milder than those grown in New Mexico. These long, slender peppers come in varieties also known as long green, long red, California, or New Mexico. Anaheims are eaten in both the green and red stages of development. When mature and red, they are often made into *ristras*. Ristras are strands of peppers that have been strung together on a cord, hung to dry, then used for cooking (and also often used in southwestern décor). Dried reds are delicious when ground into chile powder. And fresh green Anaheims are the peppers of choice for the classic Mexican dish called Chilies Rellenos (see recipe, Page 56).

Ancho: Anchos are the dried form of the Poblano Chile. Their appearance is flat, wrinkled, and heart shaped, ranging in colour from brick red to deep mahogany. Considered one of the mild to moderately hot peppers, they are extensively used in cooked sauces.

Bell Peppers: The most familiar pepper in the United States, the green, red, yellow, and orange bell peppers are sweet and delicious, carrying literally zero heat! They are crisp and firm – great in salads, stir-fries, and sauces!

Casabel: In their fresh state, casabels are green or red and shaped like a small tomato. When dried, their skin turns a rich brownish-red and becomes translucent. These peppers are sometimes referred to as "rattle chilies" or "jingle bells" because the seeds rattle when you shake them. Casabels can be classified as a moderately hot pepper and have rich, smoky undertones.

Cayenne Pepper (pronounced KI-yehn):   These peppers are long and thin with sharply pointed pods that are either straight or curled at the tip. They grow from 6" to 10" in length, are available in their green stage during the summer months, and ripen to a much hotter fire-engine red when harvested in the fall. Fresh cayennes are often used in Cajun cooking and, when dried, are commonly ground into cayenne pepper.

Cherry Pepper: Cherry peppers (so-named for their resemblance to round, red cherries) range in colour from bright red to green and are great for stuffing, pickling, and adding to sauces. Their pungency is measured from mild to moderately hot.

Chilaca (pronounced chih-LAH-kuh):   A mild, rich-flavoured pepper that, when dried, is known as the pasilla. The long, narrow chilaca often has a twisted shape. It turns from dark green to dark brown when fully mature.

Chiltepin (pronounced chill-TUH-peen):   Chiltepins grow wild in Mexico and the southwestern United States but are difficult to find because they grow on the rocky surfaces of steep slopes and are usually protected by other shrubbery. This chile is often referred to as the tepin, bird, or bird's eye peppers and, even though the smallest in size, is considered "the mother of all hot peppers"...*even hotter than the habañero, some claim* (though I could never understand why it measures so much less on the Scoville scale)! The round, berry-shaped chiltepin peppers are bright red when mature and grow upright on a large, attractive plant that can spread out up to six feet across. These peppers are good in soups, stews, beans, and sauces.

Chipotle (pronounced chee-POHT-lay):   Chipotle is not actually a name for any particular pepper, but is a process by which mature jalapeño peppers are smoked and dried. The process produces a deep, nutty/fruity flavour with tobacco and cocoa undertones and makes chipotles significantly hotter than the green jalapeño. Besides being found in their dried state, chipotles can also be purchased packed in canned adobo sauce. Great for marinades, soups, salsas, and barbecue sauces.

Fresno (pronounced FREZ-noh): Though somewhat more fiery, they are similar to the jalapeño, and also compared to, but not quite as hot as, the serrano. Fresnos are wonderful when roasted and stuffed, contribute a nice level of heat to green chile sauce, and add a delicious flavour to salsas. Green Fresnos are available in the summer, with the hotter red ones available in the fall.

Guero: Gueros are yellow-green in colour, about 3" in length and a little narrower and thinner-walled than jalapeños. They are also referred to as "blondies" in Mexico because of their yellow colour. They have a relatively mild flavour and are primarily used in salsas. You can also marinate them as in Marinated Guero Chilies (see recipe, Page 29).

Habañero (pronounced ah-bah-NEH-roh): In Spanish, habañero means "Havana like" or "from Havana", thus speculation that the pepper originated in Cuba. Its reputation as the hottest variety of chile known was once documented by Dominican priest Francisco Ximenez who, in 1722, wrote of a chile from Havana that was so fiery that just one pod would "make a bull unable to eat"! After hearing this, if you would *still* like to feel their pain, habañeros are most easily recognizable by their lantern shape and pointed ends, measuring about 1-1/2 to 2" around. They are commonly a bright orange colour but can grow to a variety of other colours including red, yellow, and white. The habañero when ripe or dried and powdered has a unique apricot scent. Compare to Scotch bonnet.

Hungarian Wax: Hungarian wax chilies are the hot version of sweet banana peppers. They are easy to grow and usually reach 5" in length, although they can reach up to 6 or 7" long, starting out canary yellow and ripening to orange or red, they are most commonly sold when yellow, either fresh or pickled in jars. May be substituted by chilies guero.

Jalapeños (pronounced holl-uh-PAIN-yo): This is probably the most familiar and popular hot pepper in America, having a decent amount of heat and a good, rich flavour. These tapered 2" long peppers are normally consumed when they are green but are sometimes available in their fully ripe, bright red stage. They are also sold canned, sliced, and pickled, and are used in a wide array of products including sausage, cheese, and jelly. Jalapeños that have been smoked and dried are referred to as chipotle peppers.

New Mexico: This pepper (also known as Anaheim) has a sweet, earthy flavor. It's mild enough to add lots of flavour to a recipe without too much heat. Dark red, dried New Mexico chilies are often seen in wreaths and ristras.

Paprika (pronounced pah-pree-kah): Paprika is a powdered reddish brown spice derived from the dried paprika pepper. It is available in sweet, mild, and hot forms. Sweet or hot Hungarian paprika is more pungent than the mild Spanish type.

Pasilla (pronounced pah-SEE-yah): The pasilla (also called chile negro), a very tasty condiment with a hint of liquorice, is the dried version of the chilaca pepper. "Pasilla", meaning "little raisin" in Spanish (though not exactly "little" at 6 to 12" long), looks black and wrinkled like a raisin! This skinny chile has a pointed end and a rich chocolate colour. Very low on the scale of heat, it is wonderful cut into strips and added to soups and casseroles. When making into a chile sauce, the pasilla adds a distinct flavour to enchiladas or marinades for pork and beef. Enjoy the mellow undertones…they are subtle and enchanting!

Pimiento (pronounced pi-MEN-toh): The pimento is a large, red, heart-shaped sweet pepper that measures 3 to 4" long and 2 to 3" wide. The flesh of the pimiento (the Spanish word for "pepper") is sweet, succulent and more aromatic than that of the red bell pepper. Pimientos are the familiar red stuffing found in green olives.

Poblano (pronounced puh-BLAH-noh): Poblano peppers (ancho when dried) are mild, heart-shaped peppers with thick walls, which, like the Anaheim, make them great for stuffing.

Rocoto: Also referred to as Locoto, Manzano, and Peron, is common to the Andes from Chile to Columbia as well as the highlands of Mexico and Central America. They are mostly grown on small family plots and are rarely seen in the United States. The seeds are dark brown or black rather than yellow or white. Under the right growing conditions, the plants will grow up to 10' tall if not subjected to extreme heat or frost. The fruit matures to yellow and is very fleshy (similar to a bell pepper). Though somewhat milder than the habañero, rocotos have a significant burn factor! *(They're **HOT**!)*

Scotch Bonnet – These peppers (also known as Bahamian, Bahama mama, Jamaican hot, or Martinique), are almost indistinguishable from the habañero except that they are a little smaller. They grow on tall, vigorous plants and bear peppers that start out green, maturing to a beautiful orange colour. They have a luscious, fruity aroma that hints of apples, cherries, and tomatoes. Native to the Caribbean, they are available in the UK in green, yellow, orange, white, brown, and red as well as multi-toned. These peppers are great for making salsas and sauces, and are right up there on the heat charts! *So, exercise caution in determining just how many to use in your cooking!*

Serrano (pronounced sur-RAH-noh): Very popular in Mexico and the southwestern United States, these small (1" to 4" long) bullet-shaped peppers are primarily consumed fresh, usually in salsas. Serranos are typically sold in their mature green state, although they are also sometimes available when red. They are considered a *very* hot pepper.

Thai: Tiny peppers, about 1-1/2" long x 1/4" diameter, ranging in colour from green to red, they incorporate an extremely hot, lingering burn. Thai peppers are very popular in Southeast Asian cooking. They can be substituted for serranos (about 1 Thai to 3 serranos).

Benefits of Eating Chilies

Chile peppers are not only *fun to eat* but are also *very good for you!* Chilies have little or no fat, cholesterol, sodium, carbohydrates, sugar, or calories! They are also high in Vitamins A, C, and E and contain folic acid, potassium, and calcium. They are actually more nutritious than most vegetables. In fact, weight-for-weight, fresh green chile peppers contain about twice as much Vitamin C as citrus fruits while red chile peppers contain more Vitamin A than carrots! Plus, eating chilies increases your heart rate - thereby increasing your metabolism, allowing you to burn more calories! ***YES !!!***

Additionally, chilies have been found to contain a natural pain reliever. For that reason, capsaicin is now indicated as an ingredient in some lozenges and headache remedies, as well as topical liniments for arthritis. Liniments may initially cause a harmless burning sensation that can be annoying to some people. Many people, though, find the slight burning, penetrating sensation somewhat pleasant. You can actually prepare your *own* arthritic remedy by making a paste of 9 parts flour, 1 part olive oil, 1 part cayenne pepper, and some water. Spread the mixture on a cloth, fold it in half, and use it on the affected area!

Chile peppers also have a reputation of easing congestion by clearing your sinuses!

And…it is theorized by some cultures that because consuming chile peppers makes you sweat, the body temperature becomes lower, thereby reducing a fever!

Oh, and as a *squirrel deterrent*, capsaicin has a *very* impressive history! Chile powder is commonly added to birdseed to prevent squirrels from intimidating the birds, eating their seeds, and destroying feeders. It seems that squirrels have extremely sensitive receptors that send intense heat and sweat messages to their brains when they eat chile peppers. But birds don't have the same receptors so they experience *no adverse effect.* In fact, the Vitamin A contained in chilies is healthy for them and brightens their plumage! It's a natural *and safe* solution to ensure that *only birds* are eating from your feeders!

In summary, while spicing up a hum-drum menu, the versatile chile can make you healthy, enliven your home with colourful ristras, and brighten the fading feathers of a goldfinch! In fact, chilies are so beloved that their images can be found *(almost anywhere!)* on everything from potholders and kitchen magnets to neckties and boxer shorts!

And*, last, but <u>certainly</u> not least, chile peppers make us HAPPY!

Capsaicin Tolerance and "Addiction"

*Believe it or not…*some lean toward the belief that the pungent little fruit has certain addictive qualities, as it is possible to build up a tolerance for the heat in chile peppers!

*This is how it goes, folks!…..*The capsaicin oil in the chilies irritates the pain receptor cells in the mouth, nose, and throat. When the nerves in these areas experience the pain created by the capsaicin, they send out messages of pain to the brain. The brain then responds by releasing endorphins (the body's natural painkiller). Not only do these endorphins act as a painkiller, but at the same time, they create a temporary feeling of *euphoria, giving the Chile Head a natural "high!"*

Not to be confused with an addiction in the *true sense of the word:* Even though a craving for chilies can occur, *it never becomes a physical necessity:* There is no loss of control in eating chilies. There is no withdrawal (though we may *miss* them, we *don't get sick* if we don't *have* them!). And though tolerance to higher heat levels can increase over time, we don't *need* increasing amounts to feel normal. *(We're just **normal 'ole Chile Heads**!)*

So, there you go! A natural high with none of the negatives of a "true" addiction!

A Word of Caution: CALIENTE! (HOT!)

Yes...it's a word of caution to any aspiring Chile Head! ... Whenever working with chile peppers, certain precautions need to be taken to avoid chile pepper irritation. If the capsaicin contained in the inner flesh and seeds comes into contact with your skin or eyes, the burning will be <u>*very painful*</u>. Always (*I repeat, always*!) wear thin latex gloves when handling chile peppers. And **don't touch your face, eyes, or any other "vital body parts"** until you've removed the gloves and washed your hands thoroughly with warm soapy water. If you are too stubborn to follow this all-important step...you **really** might want to reconsider working with hot peppers and should probably give up the idea!

If you continue your *"burning desire"* to work with hot chilies and your hands *should* for some reason come in contact with the peppers, wash them with rubbing alcohol and then warm soapy water. That should help!

Some people claim to wear a facemask or handkerchief over their nose and mouth in order to avoid inhaling the "hot" fumes of the peppers. This may seem extreme, but it actually is *not* a bad idea – particularly if you're working with *a lot* of chilies for an extended period of time! ... Or, if you are roasting hot chilies or cooking them in a *poorly ventilated area*, you might want to follow this advice! ... **not kidding**, when you cook hot chilies, they spew forth fumes that can cause you to *cough*, and **cough**, and ***cough!***

In the event you bite into a pepper that is too hot, *pleeeease...don't try to put the fire out with water*! (Capsaicin is not soluble in water and only makes the heat spread to other areas of your mouth and throat.) Instead, milk or yogurt might help. If these foods don't work or are unavailable, try a piece of bread. Bread will act like a sponge in absorbing some of the heat. Another remedy is to swish and gargle with VODKA *(yes, I said **vodka**!!)*, since capsaicin is soluble in alcohol *(My recommendation is to spit it out after doing so, though - if you swallow enough of it, you may be cashing in your chile burn for a headache!)* Another solution to an unpleasant encounter with a hot pepper might be to swish, gargle, and spit with hydrogen peroxide. (You can also hold a paper towel soaked with hydrogen peroxide up to your lips to ease the burn.) If these remedies don't work, fear not! After a few minutes, the heat from the chile will cause you to break into a sweat ... and you will cool down naturally! *...Or...my favorite antidote is to just eat another chile (**or two**)!!!*

Availability of Chilies

Grown in California, New Mexico, and Texas (as well as imported from Mexico), fresh chile peppers are generally available year-round. If you *can't* find them fresh, dried chilies are always (dependably) available in most supermarkets, as are those that have been processed in cans or jars. I've found most produce grocers to be very accommodating in ordering a particular type of chile if you need it. *(Remember...if you don't ask, you'll never know!)*

Selecting Chilies

Fresh chile peppers should be well shaped, firm, and glossy with deep, vivid colours. Skins should be tightly drawn and unwrinkled, and the stems fresh and green. Avoid buying peppers with soft, sunken, or black spots or that are shriveled; and, with the exception of jalapeños, which typically have cracks around their stems, chile peppers should be free of anything resembling a slash or crack.

Dried chile peppers should definitely be wrinkled (*after all...they are dried!*) but should be *whole and glossy*.

How to Store, Prepare, and Peel Fresh Chilies

Store fresh chile peppers, wrapped in damp paper towels, in the refrigerator for up to three weeks. *They need to breathe!* Therefore, they *don't store well in a plastic bag*. Check the chilies once in a while for soft spots. If this occurs, either use them right away or throw them out! If you bought more than you can use, just hang them to dry in a cool, well-ventilated place. Once they've dried, chilies can be stored in an airtight container at room temperature for up to four months.

To prepare fresh chilies, remove the stem, slit lengthwise and rinse under running water, removing the inner membrane while doing so. Since the greatest majority of heat is concentrated inside the chilies, you will want to continue rinsing until all the seeds have been washed away. Soaking the peppers in cold salted water for several hours will also *somewhat* diminish the heat. Then just drain and cut, chop, or slice the peppers as directed in the recipe.

Recipe formulas sometimes call for roasted and peeled chilies. This is very easy to do! Just make a small slit in each chile near the stem so that the steam can escape. Place chilies on a baking sheet under the broiler 3 to 5" from the heat. Broil—turning chilies with tongs—until they are evenly blistered and blackened on all sides. Remove from the oven, and place in a plastic bag to steam for about 15 minutes. *This loosens the skins from the pepper, making them easier to peel.*

Another method of roasting is to use your stovetop. Just place a wire rack over an electric burner and roast the chilies, turning with tongs, until they are evenly blistered. Then...steam and peel. (You can also flame-roast chilies on a metal skewer over a gas stove...but this can be a monotonous and time-consuming effort if you're working with more than just a few peppers. I think, of all methods, I prefer broiling.)

Roasted chilies can be frozen for up to a year. It really saves a lot of time *(and money)* if you buy a large quantity of peppers, roast them, and freeze in individual packages. Besides, chilies that have been roasted and then frozen are even *easier* to peel!

Whole, fresh chilies also can be frozen. Just wash and dry them and place them in a single layer in a pan. Freeze. When solid, transfer the peppers to plastic bags for freezer storage.

Using Dried Chilies

Dried chilies are usually soaked until soft, then pureed. To soften dried chilies, place them in a pan, cover with boiling water and soak until softened (the skin may still feel papery and tough, but the pulp will be tender). Before pureeing, remove stems and seeds (or do it before soaking). Process the chilies in a blender or food processor with only enough liquid to make a paste.

Dried chilies can also be pulverized using a mortar and pestle or food processor for use as *chile* powder (with an "e") or when making *chili* powder (with an "i"). Okay…let's explain *that* one…

Chile Powder Versus Chili Powder

Chile Heads sometimes ridicule the use of so-called "chili powder" commonly found in supermarkets, only because it contains other ingredients such as garlic powder, oregano, cumin, and salt. "Chili" powder with additives such as these will be dark brown in colour; whereas, pure ground chile is a deep red and carries a full-powered thrust! So, watching the spelling of "chili" powder as opposed to (*real*) "chile" powder can be an all-important aspect to the results of your cooking! Personally, I feel chili powder has gotten some adverse publicity and most definitely has a significant place in enhancing various dishes. Therefore, you will see it included in several recipes in this book – not to mention the recipe for the *homemade version* (Page 24)!

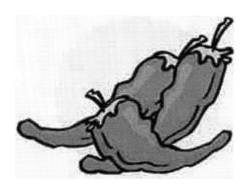

Suggested Menus
For
Family and Entertaining

- *Barbecue on the Deck*

- *Brunch Buffet*

- *Casual Friday Night Supper*

- *Chile Chili Chimi Dinner*

- *Cocktail Party with a Mexican Flair*

- *Fiesta*

- *"Vegetarian" Night*

- *Oriental Celebration*

- *Prairie Dinner on the Patio*

- *Festa Italiana*

- *South-of-the-Border Birthday Bash*

- *Spanish Banquet*

Barbecue on the Deck

Both the ribs and the corn are messy...
so my recommendation is to save this menu for an ultra casual affair
...and have plenty of napkins and wet wipes on hand!

Crab Meat Log *(26) with Thin Slices of French Bread*

Spare Ribs with Chipotle Honey Barbecue Sauce *(102)*
Ensalada Mexicana de Pastas *(49)*
Corn with Chile Lime Butter *(106)*

Sopaipillas *(122)*

* * *

Brunch Buffet

With a little advance preparation, you will be set free to
enjoy yourself when your guests arrive.
I like to use a south-of-the-border theme
with colours of red, green, and white when I set out this buffet...
Bright linen and bold-patterned platters and bowls
add to making this carefree meal delightfully festive!

A Pitcher of **Pickled Bloody Mary** *(40)*

Mexican Quiche *(61)*

Chicken Enchiladas *(72)*

Platter of Sliced Tomatoes, Green Pepper Rings, Shredded Lettuce, and Black Olives

Bowl of Sour Cream

Fried Milk *(117) with* **White Chocolate Sauce**

Casual Friday Night Supper

Fix up the salsa and get your ice cream started in the morning!

Los demás, mis amigos, son fácil!
(The rest, my friends, is easy!)

Fish Tacos *(65) on Warm Tortillas*
with **Salsa Verde** *(30) and Sour Cream*
Red Rice *(110)*

Fried Ice Cream *(116)*

* * *

Chile Chili Chimi Dinner

*Bet you can't say **that** ten times after a margarita or two!*
Doesn't matter....no one will care.
Instead, they will be enjoying your rich, flavourful chili
and your crisp and delightful chimichangas.
*Makes a great dinner ... for **any** occasion!*

Cup of Three-Chile Chili *(97)*

Fried Chicken Chimichangas *(75)*
Cinco De Mayo Guacamole *(25)*
Sour Cream
Roasted Mexican-Style Vegetables *(108)*

Sorbet

Cocktail Party with a Mexican Flair

Finger food at its best!

Assortment of Bottled Water and Mexican Beers on Ice

Three-Cheese Crab Quesadillas *(69)*
Chili Con Queso Dip *(23) with Assorted Raw Vegetables*
Señor Paul's Stuffed Mushrooms *(31)*
Taco Salad *(51)*

Mexican Wedding Cakes *(119)*

* * *

Fiesta

This is a fun and relaxing meal for entertaining...
The margaritas set the stage...the Cilantro Shrimp with Avocado whet the appetite...
And your guests get to participate by assembling their own entrée!

Perfect Margaritas *(39)*

Cilantro Shrimp with Avocado *(64)*
Served with Nacho Chips

Chicken and Beef Fajitas *(73) with Warm Tortillas*
Salsa Verde *(30)*
Shredded Lettuce and Sliced Ripe Tomato
Shredded Jack Cheese

Pumpkin Empanadas *(121) with Sweetened Whipped Cream*

"Vegetarian" Night

For Friday nights or anytime……whether or not you are a vegetarian!

Makes a beautiful presentation…
Just place the rellenos in the center of an oval plate and smother with sauce. Then spoon
some vegetable salsa along one side, and frijoles refritos along the other.

Red Bell Pepper Soup *(46) with Tortilla Chips*

Chilies Rellenos with Chilies Rellenos Sauce *(56-57)*
Vegetable Salsa *(35)*
Frijoles Refritos *(107)*

Peach Fajitas Ala-a-Mode *(120)*

* * *

Oriental Celebration

Decorate your back porch with Japanese lanterns,
use a lucky bamboo or bonsai as a centerpiece,
and break out those chopsticks!!! …Your guests will love you for it!

Saki and Green Tea

Tangy Miso Soup *(47)*

Assortment of Sashimi with Wasabi, Soy Sauce,
and Pickled Ginger (Garni)

Stir-Fried Szechuan Shrimp *(68)*
Sautéed Pea Pods
Steaming Hot White Rice

Fresh Orange Slices and Fortune Cookies

Prairie Dinner on the Patio

Light up the chiminea and torches and invite your closest friends!
This makes for a hearty meal…ending a long day out on the range!

Corona with Lime

The Mad Mexican's Dip *(33)*

Southwestern Chicken Stew *(78)*
with **Corn Bread** *(54)* and **Jalapeño Pepper Butter** *(28)*

Apple Enchilladas *(114)* and *Vanilla Ice Cream*

* * *

Festa Italiana

For a really special meal in the Italian tradition (yes…Italians like it hot!),
use a red and white checkered tablecloth and napkins,
add a good bottle of Chianti, and find some authentic Italian music.
Then, dim the lights, introduce a few candles into the picture, and…
Enjoy an absolutely delicious and romantic dinner!

Warm Italian Bread with Whipped Butter

Mixed Green Salad drizzled with basil-flavoured olive oil

Shrimp and Scallops Marinara ala Roma *(67)* over *Linguini*

Lemon Flan *(118)*

South-of-the-Border Birthday Bash

Go all out...Hang piñatas from the ceiling and buy sombreros for everyone....
Hire some mariachis or dig out a lively CD!
*Kids **love** this...but (I must tell you!) adults really get into the groove too!*

Chili-Cheese Nachos (22)

Beef Tacos (88)
Spanish Rice (111)
Platter of Sliced Cucumbers, Tomatoes, and Avocados Sprinkled with Lime Juice

Birthday Cake and Ice Cream!

* * *

Spanish Banquet

You will feel like you should be at an outdoor café on a cobblestone street in Spain...
*which is exactly where I **found** this recipe for Paella!*

Sangria (42)

Fiery Gazpacho (44)

Paella Español (66)

Caramel Flan (115)

Spicy Beginnings

- *Ancho Chile Sauce*
- *Broccoli Cheese Dip*
- *Chili-Cheese Nachos*
- *Chili Con Queso Dip*
- *Chili Powder*
- *Cinco De Mayo Guacamole*
- *Crab Meat Log*
- *Fired-Up Sausage Morsels*
- *Ancho Garlic Sauce*
- *Jalapeño Pepper Butter*
- *Roasted Garlic*
- *Marinated Guero Chilies*
- *Salsa Verde*
- *Señor Paul's Stuffed Mushrooms*
- *Stuffed Cherry Peppers*
- *The Mad Mexican's Dip*
- *Toasted Garlic Jalapeños Wrapped in Bacon*
- *Vegetable Salsa*

Ancho Chile Sauce

Anchos are dried Poblano peppers that are relatively low in heat on the Scoville Scale, adding a lot of flavour and a mild bite to this delicious formula.

*Great served as a sauce or marinade for pork and poultry and absolutely perfect when used in making **Stir-Fried Szechuan Shrimp** (68)!*

4 dried Ancho chilies
1 cup onion, coarsely chopped
3 cloves garlic
1 tablespoon white vinegar

1 teaspoon fresh chopped oregano (or 1/4 teaspoon dried, crushed)
1/4 teaspoon cumin
1/2 cup chicken broth

Soak chilies in hot water for 30 minutes. Drain. Discard stems and seeds.

Place chilies in a blender or food processor with remaining ingredients. Puree.

Transfer mixture to a small saucepan and bring to a boil. Reduce heat, cover, and simmer for 20 minutes.

Makes about 1 Cup

This sauce will keep for several weeks when refrigerated. Or, place equal portions into an ice cube tray, freeze, then pop them out into a zippered freezer bag. They will be set to go when you are!

Broccoli Cheese Dip

Bueno, amigos! This will spice up your appetizer table!

1 16-ounce bag frozen chopped broccoli
1 10-3/4 ounce can cream of broccoli soup
1 16-ounce block jalapeño pepper cheese, cut
  up in small cubes

1 16-ounce block garlic cheese, cut up in small
  cubes
Nacho chips

Cook broccoli according to package directions. Drain, squeezing out excess liquid.

Process broccoli and undiluted soup in a blender until broccoli is very fine.

Turn broccoli mixture into an ovenproof casserole and stir in cheeses.

Place in a 350-degree oven for about 20 minutes or until cheeses are melted. Stir well to blend and serve with nacho chips.

Serves 8 to 10

Chili-Cheese Nachos

Easy to make and a great crowd-pleaser!

1-pound can chili con carne with beans
1-pound can refried beans
1 box flat, round nacho chips

2 ounces canned jalapeño peppers (drained)
16-ounce package shredded Monterey Jack
   cheese

Heat chili and refried beans in a medium-size saucepan, stirring constantly until mixture comes to a boil.

Arrange nachos on baking sheets and spoon a teaspoon full of the chili mixture onto each.

Arrange jalapeño peppers over nachos and sprinkle with cheese.

Place under the broiler about 6" from heat *(watch carefully!)* until cheese is melted.

Arrange on individual serving dishes or a large platter.

A terrific appetizer or snack!

Serves 6 to 8

Chili Con Queso Dip

Ole'! El mejor!
(Bravo! The best!)

1-pound can cheddar cheese sauce
1-pound can chili con carne (with or
   without beans)

1 teaspoon *(or more!)* **hot sauce**
Tortilla chips

Combine cheese sauce and chili in a 1-1/2 quart microwave casserole. Stir in hot sauce. Cover and heat in microwave until hot, stirring occasionally.

To serve, place casserole on a large serving plate and surround with tortilla chips for dipping.

Serves 6 to 8

Translated, "con queso" means "with cheese".

Chili Powder

*Not to be confused with "**chile**" (which is pure ground hot chilies),
"**chili**" powder is a combination of ground chilies and other spices
that not only incorporate distinct flavours, but also tame the heat of the chile peppers!*

2 tablespoons paprika   1-1/4 teaspoon ground cumin
1-1/4 teaspoon cayenne pepper   1-1/4 teaspoon garlic powder
2 teaspoons oregano powder   3/4 teaspoon onion powder

Mix together and store in a tightly lidded jar!

Makes 1/4 Cup

Use for flavouring chili con carne and other stews and sauces.

Cinco De Mayo Guacamole

*Used primarily as a condiment for many Mexican and Southwestern foods,
guacamole (pronounced gwahk-a-MOLE-ee)
has a creamy texture and, when spiced up just right, the avocados wake up with flavour!
(Guacamole is also great when served as a dipper with tortilla chips!)*

3 ripe avocados
1 small red onion, diced
2 jalapeño chile peppers (seeds and
   membranes removed), diced
1/4 cup chopped fresh cilantro

Juice of 1 lime
1/2 teaspoon hot sauce
1 small ripe tomato, diced
Salt and freshly ground black pepper

Peel and quarter avocados. Discard pits.

Mash avocado with a fork in a medium-sized bowl. Set aside.

Place onion, jalapeño peppers, cilantro, lime juice, hot sauce, and tomato in a blender container.
Puree until smooth.

Add pureed mixture to avocados. Stir. Add salt and pepper to taste.

Cover and refrigerate for one hour before serving.

Makes about 1-1/2 Cup

*Cinco De Mayo (pronounced SEENG-koh-duh-MAH-yoh), means 5th of May which is a holiday
observed by communities in Mexico (and by Mexican-American communities in the United States)
in commemoration of the defeat of French troops at the Battle of Puebla in 1862.*

Crab Meat Log

This will make even a "crabby" friend smile!

8 ounces cream cheese, softened
2 cherry peppers (seeds and membrane
   removed), very finely chopped
2 teaspoons minced onion
2 teaspoons minced fresh parsley
1/2 teaspoon Worcestershire sauce

1/4 cup finely chopped celery
6-ounce can crab meat, drained and flaked (all
   traces of membrane removed)
1/3 cup finely-chopped walnuts
2 pieces of Romaine lettuce hearts
Crackers or French bread slices

Cream together cream cheese, cherry peppers, onion, parsley, and Worcestershire sauce. Add celery and crabmeat and blend well.

Form mixture into the shape of a log and roll in chopped walnuts to coat.

Cover with plastic wrap and chill for several hours or overnight.

Place two pieces of Romaine lettuce hearts lengthwise on a rectangular or oval plate, leafy side of each turned toward outer edges of plate *(for aesthetics!)* and place crab roll on top.

Serve with crackers or French bread slices.

Serves 6

Fired-Up Sausage Morsels

Looking for a "hot fix?"   This'll do it, "Baby!"

*These little appetizers are **NOT** for the weak or meek…
but they **ARE muy** delicioso!!! (… that's "**very** delicious"… !)*

Ancho Garlic Sauce *(Recipe below)*
1 pound finely-ground hot sausage
1/2 teaspoon crumbled dried sage
1/2 teaspoon crumbled dried oregano
1-1/2 cups grated sharp cheddar cheese

1 tablespoon hot sauce
6 jalapeño chile peppers (seeds and membrane
   removed), very finely chopped
1 cup biscuit mix

Prepare Ancho Garlic Sauce.

Place remaining ingredients in a mixing bowl and blend well. Form balls (about the size of a golf ball) and place in a heavy skillet.

Brown well on all sides. Drain and discard any fat.

Transfer morsels to Ancho Garlic Sauce and simmer for 30 minutes.

Using a slotted spoon to drain off most of the sauce, transfer morsels to a serving dish and pierce with colourful party picks. Serve sauce on the side for *dipping!*

Makes 1-1/2 dozen

Ancho Garlic Sauce

1/4 cup Ancho Chile Sauce (20)
1-pound can tomato puree

4 cloves garlic, minced
1 teaspoon crumbled dried oregano

Prepare Ancho Chile Sauce.

In a medium-size pot, combine Ancho Chile Sauce with remaining ingredients. Bring to a boil, stirring constantly. Reduce heat, cover, and simmer for 20 minutes.

Jalapeño Pepper Butter

*Try slathering this butter on hot **Corn Bread** (54)...Yum!*
But it's also great for sautéing flour tortillas
And other "sautéables" such as mushrooms or onions!

2 teaspoons mashed Roasted Garlic *(Recipe below)*
1/2 cup butter, softened

2 jalapeño chile peppers (seeds and membrane removed), minced
2 teaspoons fresh cilantro, finely chopped

Roast garlic.

Blend all ingredients.

Place in a small ramekin, cover and refrigerate until ready to use!

Makes about 1/2 Cup

Roasted Garlic

1 head of garlic
2 teaspoons extra-virgin olive oil

Coarsely ground salt and pepper
1/4 teaspoon oregano

Heat oven to 375 degrees.

Cut garlic in half crosswise. Place each half, cut-side up, onto a terra cotta roasting pot or onto a piece of aluminum foil.

Combine olive oil, salt and pepper, and oregano. Drizzle over garlic.

Cover with pot lid or foil.

Bake for 50 minutes. Remove from oven and cool slightly. Squeeze garlic from parchment into a small dish and mash.

Marinated Guero Chilies

*These fabulous soy-and lime-marinated chilies team up with almost **any** of your favorite foods.*
Try them on a gigantic, juicy hamburger…
or wrap them in warm tortillas along side Fish Tacos (65).

1 dozen fresh guero chile peppers
2 tablespoons vegetable oil
4 thin slices of onion, separated into rings
1/4 teaspoon garlic salt

Freshly ground black pepper
2 tablespoons extra-virgin olive oil
3 tablespoons reduced sodium soy sauce
1 tablespoon fresh lime juice

Slice chilies in half lengthwise, remove stem, seeds, and membrane. Rinse away any seed residue and pat dry with paper towels.

Pour vegetable oil in a heavy skillet over medium-high heat. When the oil is hot, add the chilies and onion and sauté until the chilies start to blister and the onions are soft and brown. Remove the pan from the heat and season with garlic salt and pepper.

In a medium-size bowl, combine the olive oil, soy sauce, and lime juice. Mix well. Add the chilies and onions and turn several times to coat well. Cover the bowl, refrigerate, and allow to marinate for at least 6 hours before serving.

Serves 6 to 12

Marinated Guero Chilies keep well in a tightly sealed jar for up to 2 weeks.

Salsa Verde

*The Hungarian wax chilies give this salsa a mildly hot zing,
making it an appropriate condiment for almost any southwestern or Mexican dish.
Or, simply serve with chips for dipping!*

1 pound tomatillos, husks removed, chopped
1/2 cup diced white onion
2 cloves garlic, minced
3 Hungarian wax chilies (seeds and ribs removed), finely chopped

Sugar to taste
Salt to taste
1/4 cup chopped fresh cilantro

Combine the tomatillos, onion, garlic, and chilies in a small, heavy saucepan and heat over medium heat until the tomatillos start to soften. Reduce the heat to low and continue cooking for a couple of minutes until the tomatillos are soft, but still colourful. Add a small amount of sugar and salt to taste. Stir.

Put the mixture in a blender or food processor and whirl for a few seconds.

Transfer the salsa to a bowl, stir in the cilantro, and cool. Cover and chill in the refrigerator for several hours before serving.

Makes about 2 Cups

This condiment is also sometimes referred to as Green Tomatillo (pronounced toh-mah-TEE-yoh) Sauce. Tomatillos (Mexican husk "tomatoes") are actually not tomatoes at all...and don't taste or smell like tomatoes either! Their flavour is tangy and tart with subtle citrus undertones. They resemble small green tomatoes and are encased in a papery husk. Tomatillos are good eaten raw, but briefly cooking them enhances their overall flavour. They are generally available from May through November, but I've also found them in supermarkets in January and February. If you can't find them fresh, you may want to check a specialty market for those that have been canned or frozen...not as good, but when you're in a pinch, they will do!

Señor Paul's Stuffed Mushrooms

Paul's favorite! And everyone else's !!!
Fabulously delicious.

1 pound bulk hot sausage
18 large white mushrooms
1/8 teaspoon ground cumin
1 Scotch bonnet chile pepper, seeds and ribs
   removed, finely diced

1/4 cup finely chopped bell pepper(*any
   colour!*)
2 cups shredded cheddar cheese

Preheat oven to 450 degrees.

Fry sausage until nicely browned. Drain off and discard all fat. Cool.

Meanwhile, remove stems from mushrooms. Reserve caps and chop stems fine. Set aside.

When sausage has cooled, crumble with fingers. Sprinkle with cumin. Add chopped mushroom stems, peppers, and cheese. Stir to combine.

Stuff mushroom caps with sausage filling, heaping to make a mound. Arrange on a broiler pan or a rack which has been placed in a baking pan and bake for 10 to 12 minutes or until tops are golden brown.

Serves 6 to 9

Stuffed Cherry Peppers

A traditional Italian favorite!!!
Serve alone, as part of an antipasto platter, or with sandwiches or hamburgers.
These colourful little gems also act as a lively companion
for pasta, grilled steak, and chicken.

20 red or green cherry peppers (or a combination of both)
White vinegar as needed
20 garlic cloves, peeled
1/3 pound extra sharp provolone cheese, cut in 1/2" cubes

1/4 pound prosciutto, sliced very thin, cut in strips
1 tablespoon black peppercorns
Extra-virgin olive oil as needed

Using latex gloves (and a face mask if you are bothered by hot pepper fumes), stem, core, and seed peppers. Place in a large pot or bowl and pour in vinegar to cover. Cover with a lid and set aside for at least 24 hours.

Slice garlic cloves in half and place in a small pot. Add one cup of water and boil for 10 minutes. Drain. Pour white vinegar over garlic to coat. Set aside for 24 hours.

Drain peppers and garlic of all vinegar (do not rinse).

For each pepper, place a slice of garlic on each side of a provolone cube. Wrap in a thin strip of prosciutto. Stuff into the center of the pepper. Repeat until all peppers have been stuffed.

Pack peppers in a jar or jars alternately with peppercorns. Drizzle with extra-virgin olive oil until the oil oozes between the peppers to the bottom of the jar(s) and the peppers are completely covered with oil. Seal jar(s) tightly and store in the refrigerator for up to two weeks.

Serves 8 to 10

The easiest way to core cherry peppers is to use a good-quality apple corer that can be found in any gourmet cooking shop.

The Mad Mexican's Dip

Easy and always a hit…serve at your next backyard barbecue!
Of course, any Mad Mexican also packs his Mylanta!!!

8-ounce package cream cheese
1-pound can chili (with or without beans)
8-ounce jar salsa (mild, medium, or hot)

8 ounces Monterey Jack cheese, shredded
Tortilla chips

Spread cream cheese in the bottom of an 8" x 8" pan. Distribute chili over cream cheese. Pour on salsa, spreading with a spoon. Sprinkle cheese evenly over top.

Bake at 375 degrees until cheese is nicely browned (about 20 minutes).

Serve hot with tortilla chips for dipping.

Serves 6

Toasted Garlic Jalapeños Wrapped in Bacon

Delicioso, mi amigo
(Delicious, my friend!)

*And, "SI!", they're **HOT**...but the longer you cook these peppers, the milder the taste.*

To make party preparation easier,
put these little tidbits together in the morning
and store in your refrigerator until it's time to cook them!

24 large fresh green jalapeño chile peppers,
seeds and ribs removed, minced
Salt water
About 1-1/2 to 2 *heads* garlic, separated into
cloves, peeled, and finely diced

2 tablespoons extra-virgin olive oil
8 ounces cream cheese, softened
12 slices bacon, cut in half

With a sharp knife, make one lengthwise slice into each jalapeño *(do not cut through!)*. Remove stems, seeds, and membranes. Place pepper pods in a bowl of cold, salted water for about an hour. Rinse and drain.

Meanwhile, sauté garlic in oil until lightly toasted, stirring occasionally to prevent scorching.

When garlic has cooled, place in a medium-size bowl, add cream cheese, and blend well.

Fill jalapeño halves with as much cream cheese mixture as they will hold. Close peppers, wipe off any cream cheese that may have oozed out, and wrap each pepper in a piece of bacon. Secure with toothpicks.

Place peppers in a large skillet over medium heat. Turn as needed to cook evenly. When done, bacon should be crisp and jalapeños should be soft and slightly browned.

Drain on paper towels. Remove and discard picks and arrange on a serving platter.

Serves 6

Legend has it that the Incas created a wall of smoke between themselves and the conquering Spaniards by burning hot peppers. The fumes created natural irritants that temporarily blinded their invaders. (So why would anyone consider resorting to nuclear weapons?!?)

Vegetable Salsa

Prepare this salsa according to your tolerance for heat…
2 teaspoons of hot sauce for medium…4 teaspoons (or more) for hot!

For longer storage, transfer to sterilized canning jars
and process until the lids have sealed!
(Makes a great gift when the jars are topped off with colourful fabric tied with a ribbon.
…you may even want to include a small envelope with a copy of the recipe inside…)

5 pounds fresh, ripe tomatoes, coarsely chopped
1 tablespoon sugar
1 tablespoon salt
5 tablespoons cornstarch mixed with 5 tablespoons cold water
2 cups chopped red onion

1 cup chopped celery
1 cup chopped green bell pepper
1 cup canned corn, drained
1 cup chopped cilantro
2 teaspoons cumin powder
2 teaspoons *(or more!)* hot sauce
1/2 teaspoon salt

In a heavy pot, combine the tomatoes, sugar, and 1 tablespoon of salt. Bring to a boil, stirring. Reduce heat and simmer (uncovered) for 30 minutes.

Stir in cornstarch/water mixture. Continue cooking for about 2 minutes, stirring. Remove from heat.

Blend tomato mixture with a hand mixer until it resembles a chunky puree.

Add red onion, celery, green bell pepper, corn, cilantro, cumin, hot sauce, and 1/2 teaspoon of salt. Stir.

When cool, transfer to a tightly sealed container and refrigerate.

Makes About 2 Quarts

Cilantro (the leaves from the coriander plant) resembles flat Italian parsley and is commonly used in Middle Eastern, Mediterranean, Indian, Latin American, and Southeast Asian cooking. Both the cilantro leaves and the coriander seeds are known to have various medicinal benefits and are widely used in soothing digestive problems and controlling infection.

Beverages for the Brave

❑ *Molotov Cocktail*

❑ *Perfect Margaritas*

❑ *Pickled Bloody Mary*

❑ *Prairie Oyster*

❑ *Sangria*

Molotov Cocktail

The meaning of true danger: A Molotov Cocktail in your hand!

*It's **dynamite**!*

1-1/2 ounce Russian vodka   Splash of white rum
4 dashes of hot sauce

Place a bottle of Russian vodka in the freezer overnight. Shake the hot sauce into the bottom of an old fashion glass. Add vodka, stir, and splash with white rum. *Drink*!

Makes 1 Drink

The name Molotov cocktail is derived from Vyacheslav Mikhailovich Molotov, Soviet Minister for Foreign Affairs from 1939 to 1949. At the onset of World War II, Finland refused to allow the Soviet Union to establish military bases in their country. The Soviets attacked in retaliation in what became known as the Winter War (1939-1940). The outnumbered and poorly equipped Finnish Army (oddly enough) borrowed an explosive device from Soviet-backed Spanish Republican defenders of Madrid in the Spanish Civil War, dubbing the device "Molotov Cocktail". It was only after Molotov added salt to the womb by publicly denying that the Soviet Union was bombing Finland, but rather delivering food to their starving people, that the Finns responded by "greeting" the advancing Soviet tanks with the Molotov Cocktails!

Perfect Margaritas

Wedge of lime
Sea salt
6 ounces premium tequila

4 ounces cointreau or triple sec
Juice of 2 lemons
Juice of 2 limes

Prepare four margarita glasses by running the lime wedge around the rims and then dipping the rims into a plate that has been sprinkled very liberally with salt.

Pour tequila, cointreau, and juice of lemons and limes into the container of a blender. Add a generous portion of ice and process until well chilled.

Strain into prepared glasses.

Makes 4 Drinks

So what exactly is a "perfect" margarita? Ask 100 bartenders and you may well get 100 different answers. They will (unanimously) say that it contains tequila, triple sec, and lime or lemon...but what proportions of each ingredient should you use?

Truth is, there is no "right" or "wrong" way to make margaritas! Try this recipe...and if it doesn't suit you...use your creative "juices" to mix up the proportions that are right for your individual taste! (Just follow one rule and you can't go wrong...use enough tequila so that it can be tasted – but not so much that will knock you out!)

Pickled Bloody Mary

The best version of a Bloody Mary I've ever tasted!

3 ounces vodka
1-1/4 cup tomato juice
1 teaspoon garlic powder
1 tablespoon freshly squeezed lemon juice

1 teaspoon Worcestershire sauce
A few splashes of hot sauce
2 celery stalks
Pickled garlic

In a pitcher, combine vodka, tomato juice, garlic powder, lemon juice, Worcestershire, and hot sauce. Add a cup of ice cubes and stir until mixture is icy cold.

Strain into glasses. Add a stalk of celery. Thread pickled garlic on a toothpick and rest over the top.

Makes 2 Drinks

Prairie Oyster

1 teaspoon Worcestershire Sauce
A few drops of hot sauce
1 tablespoon tomato juice

1 raw egg yolk
4 dashes of garlic-flavoured vinegar
A few dashes of cayenne pepper

Pour ingredients (in order of list) into a wineglass. Use caution in not breaking the egg.

Shoot it!

Makes 1 Drink

Caution from the American Egg Board: *"There have been warnings against consuming raw or lightly cooked eggs on the grounds that the egg may be contaminated with Salmonella, bacteria responsible for a type of food poisoning. Healthy people need to remember there is a very small risk. Use only properly refrigerated, clean, sound-shelled, fresh, Grade AA or A eggs."*

Sangria

Sangria, a red wine punch, was originally created in Spain.
...a perfect warm-weather drink...

2 4/5-quart bottles Rioja (red Spanish wine)
4 shots white rum
20 ounces club soda
Juice of 2 limes
1 orange, seeded and sliced

1 lemon, seeded and sliced
Sugar to taste
Ice cubes
Mint sprigs, seeded orange slices, and
    Maraschino cherries for garnish

Combine the wine, rum, soda, lime juice, and sliced orange and lemon in a large pitcher. Add sugar and stir. Chill.

To serve, strain Sangria into glasses filled with ice cubes. Garnish with mint sprigs, orange slices, and cherries.

Serves 8 to 12

Tantalizing, Taste-Bud-Tingling Soups, Salads, and Breads

<u>Soups</u>

- *Fiery Gazpacho*
- *Poblano Potato Chowder*
- *Red Bell Pepper Soup*
- *Tangy Miso Soup*

<u>Salads</u>

- *Avocado Salad*
- *Ensalada Mexicana de Pastas*
- *Stuffed Campari Tomatoes*
- *Taco Salad*
- *Roasted Vegetable and Shrimp Salad in Tortilla Bowls*

<u>Breads</u>

- *Casabel and Red Bell Pepper Baguette*
- *Corn Bread*

Fiery Gazpacho

*This devilishly delightful gazpacho
is much spicier (and hotter!) than any traditional Spanish version you might try.
If you're into mellower tastes,
don't hesitate to cut back on the hot sauce and/or use chicken broth in place of the V-8!*

*By all means, though, have fun experiencing the preparation!
I like to "get-sloppy-in-the-kitchen" when making gazpacho....
You don't have to do anything perfect...
You don't need to "mince" or "dice in .25555 inch cubes!"
Just throw chunks of veggies into the blender and let it work its magic!*

3 cups Spicy Hot V-8 juice
1 cucumber, peeled, seeded, and cut up
1 red onion, peeled and quartered
2 medium-sized ripe tomatoes, cored and
    quartered
1/2 cup fresh parsley leaves (stems removed)
3 cloves garlic, peeled

3 tablespoons extra virgin olive oil
2 tablespoons raspberry or red wine vinegar
1 tablespoon Worcestershire sauce
1 teaspoon hot sauce
Garnish: unflavoured croutons, small
    cucumber cubes, and sour cream
Suggested Accompaniment: Corn Bread (54)

Place all of the ingredients (except garnish) in a blender and process until thoroughly pureed. (You may need to do this in a couple of batches to prevent overflow.)

Chill (until *really* cold!).

Ladle the gazpacho into bowls and top with croutons, cucumber cubes, and dollops of sour cream.

Serves 6

Poblano Potato Chowder

This is a dieter's nightmare…
so you'd better steer clear if you're counting calories and/or cholesterol!

But…oh, my!!!! It is soooo good!

1/2 pound bacon
1 tablespoon bacon fat
1 cup thinly sliced carrots
1 cup stemmed and seeded poblano chilies,
  chopped
1 cup chopped onion
1/4 teaspoon cayenne pepper
1/2 teaspoon cumin
3 garlic cloves, minced
4 cups chicken broth

5 cups washed (unpeeled) potatoes, diced
1/2 teaspoon salt
1/3 cup flour
2-1/2 cups whole milk
4 ounces pepper Jack cheese, shredded or cut
  into small chunks
4 ounces sharp cheddar cheese, shredded or cut
  into small chunks
2/3 cup chopped green onion

Cook bacon until crisp. Drain on paper towels. *(Reserve 1 tablespoon of fat.)* Crumble bacon and set aside.

Place a large pot over medium-low heat. Add bacon fat, carrots, poblanos, onion, cayenne, cumin, and garlic. Sauté (stirring occasionally) for about 3 minutes.

Stir in broth, potatoes, and salt. Bring to a boil. Cover, reduce heat, and simmer for about 10 minutes, or until carrots and potatoes are tender.

Meanwhile, combine a small amount of milk with flour in a saucepan. Gradually add the rest of the milk and cook, stirring occasionally, over medium heat until thickened. Remove from heat and add cheeses, stirring until melted.

Add cheese sauce to potato mixture, stir to blend, and simmer *(uncovered)* for 10 to 15 minutes.

Serve in bowls topped with green onions and crumbled bacon.

Serves 10

Red Bell Pepper Soup

With zero heat in the red bells,
the Anaheims measuring in at a very low heat level,
and the sweet bite of paprika,
this soup is meant for anyone wanting to experience a rich soup with a mild chile flavour.

9 medium-sized bell red peppers , cored, seeded, and cut up in 1/2" cubes
2 Anaheim peppers , cored, seeded, and chopped fine
2 teaspoons minced garlic
3 tablespoons extra-virgin olive oil
5 cups vegetable broth

1 cup chopped celery
1 teaspoon paprika
1 bay leaf
1/4 cup chopped fresh parsley
1/16 teaspoon powdered thyme
3 small potatoes, peeled and diced
2 cups heavy cream

In a large pot, sauté peppers and garlic in olive oil for about 3 minutes, stirring occasionally.

Add broth, celery, paprika, bay leaf, parsley, thyme, and potatoes. Stir, bring to a boil, and simmer for 10 minutes (or until potatoes are tender).

Remove and discard bay leaf. Add cream. Stir and heat to just under boiling *(do not boil).*

Serve and *enjoy!*

Serves 6

Tangy Miso Soup

Traditionally very mild in flavour,
this particular version of Miso Soup is comparatively very spicy.
A staple of Japanese cuisine,
Miso Soup is normally served with nearly every meal in Japan...including breakfast!
It is very simple to make, full of nutrients, and low in calories.

1 tablespoon sesame oil
1/2 cup sliced scallions (with green tops)
2-1/2 cups beef bouillon
1/2 cup hot water

2 tablespoons brown rice miso paste
1 teaspoon hot sauce
1/2 cake tofu, cut into 1/2" cubes
4 large white mushrooms, thinly sliced

Heat oil in the bottom of a small pot. Add green onion and cook for a minute or two, stirring frequently.

Add bouillon to pot and bring to a boil.

Meanwhile, dissolve miso paste in 1/2 cup of hot water. Add to pot and stir.

Add hot sauce, tofu, and mushrooms. Heat through and serve.

Serves 4

Miso is a thick, fermented paste made from soybeans and is frequently used in Japanese cooking. You can find it in the refrigerated section of Asian grocery stores, natural food stores, and some larger supermarkets. It comes in a variety of strengths and colours - with white being the mildest, stepping up to red, and then (the tangiest!) brown.

Avocado Salad

Cool, light, and refreshing!!!

4 avocados
Romaine lettuce leaves
1/2 cup extra virgin olive oil
3 tablespoons wine vinegar
2 cloves garlic, minced

1 teaspoon fresh thyme leaves
1 teaspoon fresh oregano, chopped
3/4 teaspoon salt
1/2 teaspoon white pepper
1/8 teaspoon cayenne pepper

Cut the avocados in half and discard the pit. Scoop out the avocado meat with a melon baller.

Arrange avocado balls on individual lettuce-lined plates.

In a small bowl, combine remaining ingredients and whisk together. Drizzle over the avocados, and serve.

Serves 4

*Avocados must reach full maturity before they are picked...but they don't soften on the tree **after** ripening. As a matter of fact (and interest!), the tree can actually be used for storing the fruit for several months after avocados reach maturity. (They keep much better on the tree than on the shelf!)*

Ensalada Mexicana de Pastas

Translated, this means Mexican Pasta Salad.
The dish is quick, easy, and refreshing...
And, best of all, it's one of those "make-aheads" that works well
from buffet dinners to backyard barbecues!
...Quick, easy, and satisfying...

8-ounces rotini pasta
15-ounce can whole kernel corn, drained
15-ounce can black beans, rinsed and drained
1/2 large red onion, chopped
2 large bell peppers, chopped (whatever colour you like...or a combination of red, green, yellow, orange)

1 cup shredded raw broccoli
1 large tomato, chopped
2 tablespoons extra-virgin olive oil
2 tablespoons fresh lime juice
1/2 cup chopped fresh cilantro
3 cloves garlic, minced
1/2 teaspoon black pepper

Cook pasta al dente. Turn into a colander and place under cold running water to cool. Drain and transfer to a medium-size bowl.

Combine remaining ingredients in a separate bowl. Stir well. Add to pasta and fold until all ingredients are well blended.

Cover and refrigerate for at least 4 hours before serving.

Serves 6

Stuffed Campari Tomatoes

Small firm and sweet tomatoes
stuffed with a colourful mixture of finely chopped marinated vegetables,
and placed on an array of mixed greens!
A presentation that is both appetizing and visually pleasing!

18 campari tomatoes
3 cloves garlic, minced
1/8 cup cilantro, chopped
1/2 medium onion, finely chopped
1 medium red bell pepper, seeded and finely
   chopped

1 Hungarian wax chile , seeds and ribs
   removed, finely chopped
1/2 small zucchini, finely chopped
3/4 cup balsamic vinegar salad dressing
Salt and pepper
Mixed salad greens with arugula

Using a sharp knife, take a small slice from the bottom of each tomato. (This will allow them to set securely on a plate.) Slice off tomato tops. Using a melon baller, scoop out interior pulp. (You can reserve the pulp and slices for a sauce, stew, or bruschetta.) Place tomatoes upside-down on paper towels to drain.

Meanwhile, in a medium bowl, combine garlic, cilantro, onion, peppers, and zucchini with salad dressing. Add salt and pepper to taste. Refrigerate for 1 hour, stirring occasionally.

Stuff tomatoes with marinated mixture, heaping as high as you can.

Arrange tomatoes on individual salad plates that have been lined with greens. Garnish greens with any remaining marinated vegetables.

Enjoy!

Serves 6

Taco Salad

A popular Mexican favorite. Great for parties or potluck barbecues!

16-ounce can refried beans (or **Frijoles Refritos** 107)
3-1/2 ounce can jalapeño peppers , finely chopped
8-ounce jar taco sauce
8-ounce package shredded Monterey Jack cheese
16-ounce carton sour cream

1/2 teaspoon salt
1/4 teaspoon pepper
1/2 teaspoon garlic powder
1 16-ounce can black pitted olives, sliced
1 cup shredded lettuce
1 cup tomatoes, diced
Nacho Chips

Spread beans in a 9 x 13" pan. Arrange jalapeño peppers over beans. Pour taco sauce evenly over peppers. Sprinkle evenly with cheese.

In a small bowl, combine sour cream with spices and spread mixture over cheese. Top with olives, shredded lettuce, and diced tomatoes.

Cover and chill for 1 hour. Serve with nacho chips.

Serves 6

Roasted Vegetable and Shrimp Salad in Tortilla Bowls

Encased in cute, edible bowls,
the roasted peppers and onions combine with a delightful, tasty marinade
to give this shrimp salad a delicate yet lively flavour!

1 red bell pepper, stemmed, seeded, and cut into thin strips
1 yellow bell pepper, stemmed, seeded, and cut into thin strips
2 jalapeño peppers, stemmed, seeded, and cut into *very* thin strips
1 medium onion, cut into thin strips
1/4 cup rice wine vinegar
2 tablespoons extra-virgin olive oil
2 tablespoons lemon juice

1 teaspoon dry mustard
2 cloves garlic, minced
1/4 cup snipped green onion tops
1 teaspoon salt
1/8 teaspoon ground hot chile pepper
1/4 teaspoon ground black pepper
1 pound shrimp, cooked and peeled (tails removed)
4 8" flour tortillas
4 cups assorted greens, shredded

Preheat broiler.

Combine pepper and onion strips on a baking sheet. Place 4" from flame and *(watching carefully!)* roast until peppers begin to blister. Turn with a spatula and continue broiling until opposite side has blistered. Remove from oven and set aside.

In a large bowl, combine vinegar, olive oil, lemon juice, mustard, garlic, green onion, salt, chile pepper, and black pepper. Add roasted vegetables and shrimp. Combine and allow mixture to marinate in refrigerator for 1 hour.

Meanwhile, preheat oven to 400 degrees.

Fit flour tortillas into 4 small, round, ovenproof casseroles folding top edges to form a fluted appearance *(or use special tortilla baking molds)*. Bake for about 10 minutes until tortillas are crisp. Remove from oven and place on individual serving plates.

Remove marinated vegetables and shrimp from refrigerator and toss with greens. Arrange in tortilla "bowls" and serve!

Serves 4

Casabel and Red Bell Pepper Baguette

A tasty twist to the ordinary garlic bread!
This wonderful blend of flavours enhances meals from spaghetti and meatballs to coq au vin!

1/2 cup unsalted butter, softened
1/8 cup chopped fresh basil
Pinch of dried oregano
3 large cloves garlic
1 fresh casabel pepper (cored, seeded, and chopped)

1 red bell pepper (cored, seeded, and chopped)
One French baguette, sliced in half lengthwise and then vertically to make 6 pieces
1/8 cup shredded Monterrey Jack cheese

Put butter, basil, oregano, garlic, casabel, and bell pepper, into the container of a blender or food processor. Blend until pureed.

Spread prepared butter onto the cut sides of the baguette pieces. Place on a foil-lined baking sheet. Sprinkle with cheese.

Bake in a 400-degree oven for 5 minutes. Then broil 6" from heat until the cheese is bubbly and browns to a light golden colour.

Serves 6

Corn Bread

Exceptionally moist!
The crunch of corn!
A sweet piquancy!
and...
Easy to make!

2 eggs, beaten
8-1/2-ounce package corn muffin mix
1/3 cup canned cream-style corn
8-ounce can whole kernel corn, drained
2 teaspoons hot pepper sauce

1 jalapeño pepper (stemmed, seeded, and finely chopped)
1 cup dairy sour cream
1/3 cup butter, melted
1 cup shredded cheddar cheese
Paprika for sprinkling

Preheat oven to 350 degrees.

Butter an 8 x 8" baking pan.

Combine eggs, muffin mix, cream-style corn, whole kernel corn, hot sauce, jalapeño pepper, sour cream, butter, and cheese. Stir until blended. Turn into prepared pan. Sprinkle with paprika.

Bake for 45 minutes.

Cut into small squares and serve warm or cold.

Serves 8

... Just Chilies, Cheese, and Eggs!

- ❑ *Chilies Rellenos*
- ❑ *Chilies Rellenos Sauce*
- ❑ *Huevos Rancheros*
- ❑ *Jalapeño Chile Pasta with Sweet Red Pepper Sauce*
- ❑ *Jalapeño Grits*
- ❑ *Mexican Quiche*
- ❑ *Roasted Garlic and Jalapeño Quesadillas*

Chilies Rellenos

Chilies Rellenos (pronounced CHEE-lehs rreh-YEH-nohs)
literally translated means stuffed peppers.

*These chilies make a beautiful presentation when arranged on a plate topped with Chilies Rellenos Sauce and surrounded by colourful **Vegetable Salsa** (35) and **Frijoles Refritos** (107).*

The secret: Get those chilies hot and blistering under your broiler....

Chilies Rellenos Sauce (*Recipe next page*)
6 large Anaheim chilies
1/2 pound Monterey Jack cheese, cut up in small cubes
1 cup canola oil

1/4 cup flour
1 cup blue corn meal (or yellow if you can't get blue)
1/2 teaspoon salt
3 eggs, beaten

Prepare Chilies Rellenos Sauce.

Rinse the chilies and pat dry. Cut a small slit near the stem of each chile (to allow steam to escape). Place under the broiler (top shelf) in a 9 x 14" baking pan. *Watch closely!* When the skins start to make popping sounds and char, flip the chilies over and char the other side. Remove from oven and place in a sealed plastic bag to steam for about 5 or 6 minutes.

Remove chilies from the bag (one at a time) and peel off skin (it should come off easily after steaming).

Cut a horizontal slit through the top of each chile. Keeping the stem attached, pull out membrane and seeds.

Stuff chilies with cheese and reposition stem. (They can be refrigerated at this point until it gets closer to serving time.)

Pour oil into a large frying pan and slowly bring temperature to 375 degrees.

Meanwhile, dredge chilies in flour. Combine cornmeal and salt in a flat dish. Dip chilies in beaten eggs and roll in cornmeal to coat.

Fry chilies until crisp, turning once (about 1-1/2 minutes per side). Carefully remove from the pan with a large slotted spoon and place on paper towels to drain.

Serve immediately with Chilies Rellenos Sauce.

Serves 3 to 6

Chilies Rellenos Sauce

1 medium onion, finely sliced
3 tablespoons extra-virgin olive oil
1 28-ounce can tomatoes
1 teaspoon garlic, pressed
1/2 teaspoon salt

1/4 teaspoon pepper
1/2 teaspoon dried leaf oregano, crushed
1 teaspoon sugar
1/2 cup chicken broth

In a medium-sized saucepan, sauté onion slices in oil until well browned.

Drain tomatoes (reserving liquid) and puree in a blender or food processor with garlic.

Add pureed tomatoes, salt, pepper, oregano, sugar, and chicken broth to sautéed onion slices. Bring to a boil. Stir and cook over medium heat for 10 minutes. If sauce thickens too much, add some of the reserved tomato liquid.

Keep warm until Chilies are done.

Blue corn meal, as its name implies, is made from blue corn, the "Southwestern Beauty" which was originally grown in Central America. Known to be the most highly regarded grain of the Pueblos, the kernels produce a corn meal that is coarse and sweet with a nutty taste. Plus...the colour is pretty cool!

Huevos Rancheros

*Pronounced WHE-voos ran-CHERR-oos.
Literally translated huevos means "eggs"
and rancheros means "ranchers".*

*...a traditional Mexican breakfast dish which can be prepared with either fried or poached eggs
served on a warm flour tortilla and smothered in a spicy tomato and onion chile sauce.*

1/2 cup chopped onion
1 tablespoon extra-virgin olive oil
16-ounce can diced tomatoes with liquid
3 garlic cloves, minced
1 Serrano chile pepper (stemmed, seeded,
   ribbed), finely chopped (*use 2 if you
   want **real** heat!*)

1/8 teaspoon Chili Powder (24)
4 teaspoons extra-virgin olive oil (divided)
2 8" flour tortillas
4 eggs
1/4 cup shredded Monterey Jack cheese

In a small, heavy pot, sauté onion in 1 tablespoon of oil until brown, stirring occasionally. Add tomatoes, garlic, Serrano chile, and chili powder. Bring to a boil, stirring. Reduce heat, cover, and simmer for about 20 minutes.

When sauce is done, place a large, non-stick frying pan over medium-high heat. Add 1 teaspoon of oil and sauté a tortilla for about 30 seconds on each side. Transfer to a warm plate. Repeat with second tortilla.

Add 2 teaspoons of oil to the frying pan, and fry the eggs (*don't overcook*). Transfer two eggs to each tortilla.

Fully cover the eggs with the hot chile sauce. (*The sauce will complete the cooking process of the eggs.*)

Sprinkle with Monterey Jack and serve!

Serves 2

Jalapeño Chile Pasta with Sweet Red Pepper Sauce

The "cool" red peppers tame the spicy pasta to a civil level.
You may be pleasantly surprised - especially if you're wary of foods with a kick!

1 medium onion, finely chopped
1 clove garlic, minced
2 tablespoons extra-virgin olive oil
2 tablespoons butter
2 large red bell peppers, seeded and finely
  julienned

1 cup chicken bouillon
1/8 teaspoon ground white pepper
14-ounce package jalapeño chile pasta,
  cooked al dente and drained

Sauté onion and garlic in oil and butter until onions are soft. Add the peppers and cook for 10 minutes. Add bouillon and pepper. Bring to a boil. Cover, reduce heat, and simmer for 15 minutes.

Turn cooked pasta onto a serving platter and top with red pepper sauce.

Serves 4

Flavoured pastas can sometimes be found in large grocery store; but, typically, your best bet is to visit a gourmet specialty market.

Jalapeño Grits

A delicious accompaniment to grilled or broiled poultry, steak, or seafood.
Also works well with a salad for lunch.

32 ounces chicken broth
1-3/4 cups uncooked quick-cooking grits
1/2 cup butter
1 medium onion, chopped
3 jalapeño peppers , (seeds and ribs removed),
   diced

1 large red, orange, or yellow bell pepper,
   seeded and diced
2 garlic cloves, pressed
2 cups shredded Monterey Jack or Cheddar
   cheese
5 large eggs, lightly beaten

Butter a large ovenproof casserole.

Combine chicken broth and grits in a bowl. Set aside.

Sauté onion, peppers, and garlic in butter until tender. Add to grits with cheese and eggs. Stir.

Turn mixture into prepared casserole.

Bake, covered, at 350 degrees for 50 to 55 minutes, or until set.

Serves 8

Mexican Quiche

*This snappy version of quiche
will make an interesting addition to your appetizer or brunch table.*

*For a deep-dish quiche, double the ingredients...
The pastry recipe, however, makes enough to adequately fill a deep dish.*

9" pie pastry shell *(Recipe below)*
4-ounce can roasted green chilies, drained
    and chopped fine (reserve 1 tablespoon
    liquid)
4-ounce can jalapeño peppers, drained, and
    chopped fine

1 pound mild cheddar cheese, shredded
3 tablespoons milk
2 eggs, beaten
Cayenne pepper

Preheat oven to 350 degrees.

Prepare pastry.

Distribute green chilies and jalapeños on bottom. Cover with cheese.

Pour milk, reserved chile juice, and eggs into a small bowl. Whisk until frothy. Pour over cheese.

Bake for 40 to 45 minutes or until top is golden brown. Remove from oven and sprinkle lightly with cayenne pepper. Cool slightly and cut into wedges to serve.

Serves 6 to 8

Quiche Pastry:

1-1/8 cups flour (plus additional for rolling)
1/2 teaspoon salt

1/3 cup plus 2 tablespoons shortening
Ice cold water

Sift flour and salt together in a large bowl. Cut shortening into flour with a pastry cutter until mixture resembles coarse crumbs. Gradually sprinkle ice water over mixture, blending with a fork and adding just enough for the mixture to come together. Form into a ball, handling as little as possible. Roll out onto a lightly floured surface until the pastry fits into the pie dish with a 1" overhang. Tuck overhang under and flute edges.

Note: *Crust becomes tough if you handle it too much. Do not re-roll pastry if it breaks apart. Just patch with water-moistened fingers.*

Roasted Garlic and Jalapeño Quesadillas

Pronounced "cay-suh-DEE-yas"...
They team up well with Avocado Salad (48).

1/4 cup **Jalapeño Pepper Butter** (28)
10 6" corn tortillas
2 cups shredded Colby and Monterey Jack
  cheese blend

8-ounce can black olives, drained and sliced
  (reserve about 20 slices for garnish)
2 avocados, peeled, pitted, and sliced
Sour cream
Hot Chile Pepper (for sprinkling)

Prepare Jalapeño Pepper Butter.

Heat a large frying pan over medium heat. Add a little Jalapeño Pepper Butter. Place two tortillas in the pan. Flip after about 30 seconds. Remove from pan after another 30 seconds (or when tortillas have browned). Repeat until all tortillas have been browned.

Preheat oven to 350 degrees.

Lay 5 tortillas on a foil-lined baking sheet. Sprinkle with 1 cup of the cheese and the black olives. Layer with avocado slices and sprinkle with remaining cheese. Cover with remaining tortillas.

Bake for 15 minutes or until cheese begins to melt.

Cut in quarters. Place a dollop of sour cream and a few (reserved) sliced black olives on each. Sprinkle with chile pepper and serve!

Serves 5

Seafood to Stimulate the Senses

❑ ***Cilantro Shrimp with Avocado***

❑ ***Fish Tacos***

❑ ***Paella Español***

❑ ***Shrimp and Scallops Marinara ala Roma***

❑ ***Stir-Fried Szechuan Shrimp***

❑ ***Three-Cheese Crab Quesadillas***

Cilantro Shrimp with Avocado

Don't compromise the fresh cilantro! ...
*You will **need** it to truly experience the unique flavour of this dish!*

Whichever way you choose to serve it
... either as a first course or a summertime luncheon entrée ...
your guests will find this dish truly delightful!

3 tablespoons chopped fresh cilantro
1/2 cup catsup
1/4 cup lime juice
1 to 2 teaspoons hot pepper sauce
1 medium red onion, chopped

1 large tomato, chopped
1 pound shrimp, cooked and peeled (tails removed)
2 avocados
Tortilla chips

In a medium-sized bowl, combine cilantro, catsup, lime juice, hot pepper sauce, onion, and tomato. Add shrimp and toss. Cover and refrigerate for at least 2 hours, stirring occasionally.

Just before serving, peel avocados and remove and discard pits. Cut up in cubes and fold into marinated shrimp. Serve with tortilla chips.

Serves 4

Fish Tacos

Tasty, flaky fish wrapped in warm tortillas...
something you will want to serve often...

To top the meal off, add Marinated Guero Chilies (29)!

1-1/2 pounds skinless haddock filets
Juice of one lime plus one tablespoon (divided)
2 eggs
1/2 cup yellow corn meal
1/2 teaspoon salt
2 jalapeño peppers (stems and seeds removed)

4 8" corn tortillas
1/2 cup corn oil
1/4 cup flour
Suggested Condiments: Sour cream, shredded lettuce, diced tomatoes, and **Salsa Verde** (30)

Cut the lime in half and squeeze the juice over fish. Allow the fish to marinate while preparing the batter.

Break the eggs into a bowl and beat with a fork. Gradually add corn meal to form a thick batter. Season with salt and 1 tablespoon lime juice.

Transfer batter into a blender jar with peppers and process until peppers are pureed. Pour onto a flat plate.

Wrap tortillas in foil and place in a warm oven (300 degrees) until ready to serve.

Pour the oil into a heavy skillet and heat to 350 degrees.

Dredge fish in flour and dip in batter to coat both sides.

Fry filets in oil for about 3 minutes on each side, or until golden brown on the outside and flaky on the inside.

Transfer fish to warm tortillas and serve with condiments.

Serves 4

Paella Español

Vaya esta noche Española!
(Go Spanish tonight!)

Make sure the clams and mussels close when handling or tapping lightly.
If they fail to close, they are dead and should be discarded.

1/4 cup extra-virgin olive oil
8 chicken legs, washed and patted dry
1 large onion, diced
3 red bell peppers, diced
2 Hungarian wax chilies (stems removed, seeded, and finely chopped)
1 jalapeño pepper (stem removed, seeded, and finely minced)
5 cups chicken stock (more if needed)
1 tablespoon minced garlic

3 cups uncooked short-grain rice
1 teaspoon salt
1 teaspoon white pepper
1/4 teaspoon saffron
3 pounds tomatoes, peeled and chopped
8 Spanish (dry-cured) chorizo sausage links
16 large shrimp, peeled (tails removed or left on)
16 clams, scrubbed and rinsed
16 mussels, scrubbed and rinsed
Lemon wedges

Heat the oil in a large pot over medium heat. Add chicken and brown on all sides, in batches if necessary. Remove chicken from pot and set aside.

Add onion and peppers to the pot and cook for 5 or 6 minutes, stirring.

Add chicken stock and bring to a boil. Add the garlic, rice, salt, pepper, saffron, and tomatoes. Stir.

Return chicken pieces to the pot, cover, reduce heat, and simmer for 25 minutes.

If the pot has gotten too dry, add extra stock.

Add the Spanish chorizo, shrimp, clams, and mussels, tucking them into the rice. Cover and cook another 5 minutes, or until the shrimp are pink and clams and mussels are open. (Discard any clams and mussels that have not opened.)

Transfer to a serving platter or individual casseroles. Arrange lemon wedges on top.

Serves 8

There are two types of chorizo (pronounced Cho-REE-thoh) sausage. Spanish Chorizo is a seasoned, smoked pork sausage flavored with garlic, paprika, and other spices and is widely used in Spanish cooking. Because it is dry-cured, it can be eaten or added to dishes without cooking. Mexican Chorizo is made with fresh pork. It is also highly seasoned but, unlike the Spanish version, it must be cooked first.

Shrimp and Scallops Marinara ala Roma

*Who **says** spicy HAS to be Tex-Mex!*

You will love this combination of ingredients and subtle flavours…
*A truly **beautiful** dish!*

8 large sea scallops, rinsed
16 medium shrimp
3 tablespoons extra-virgin olive oil
6 cloves garlic, crushed
16-ounce can artichoke hearts packed in water, drained, and cut in half
28-ounce can whole Roma tomatoes with liquid
1 cup tomato juice

1/4 cup fresh parsley, chopped
1/4 cup fresh basil, chopped
2 cherry peppers (seeds and ribs removed), finely chopped
Salt and pepper
1 pound linguini, angel hair, or spaghettini, cooked al dente
10 ounces fresh baby spinach leaves, rinsed

Cut scallops in half. Peel the shrimp and remove tails. Wash and pat dry. Refrigerate until ready to use.

In a large skillet, gently sauté garlic cloves in olive oil over medium heat.

When garlic is lightly browned, add artichoke hearts, tomatoes, tomato juice, parsley, basil, and cherry peppers. Add salt and pepper to taste. Bring to a boil, reduce heat, cover, and simmer for 30 minutes.

Begin cooking pasta according to package directions.

A few minutes before pasta is done, add spinach to tomato sauce and cook until the spinach begins to wilt (about 2 minutes).

Add shrimp and scallops, cover, and cook for about 2 minutes. (When done, the shrimp will be pink and the scallops will be translucent in the center).

Serve immediately over hot pasta.

Serves 4

Stir-Fried Szechuan Shrimp

Wake up your taste buds with this sparky dish!

2 cups steaming hot white rice
2 tablespoons minced fresh ginger
3 cloves garlic, finely minced
1/4 cup snipped green onion tops
2 tablespoons Shao Hsing (rice wine)
2 tablespoons low-sodium soy sauce

1 teaspoon sugar
4 tablespoons Ancho Chile Sauce (20)
3/4 teaspoon red pepper flakes
2 tablespoons peanut oil
1-1/2 pounds large raw shrimp, shelled and
  butterflied

Begin cooking rice according to package directions.

Meanwhile, combine ginger, garlic, and green onion in a small dish. Set aside.

In a separate, small dish, combine Shao Hsing, soy sauce, sugar, chile sauce, and red pepper flakes. Set aside.

About 3 minutes before rice is done, heat the peanut oil in a wok or heavy skillet and add ginger mixture with shrimp. Stir-fry until shrimp are pink.

Quickly stir in Shao Hsing mixture.

Fluff rice with a fork and transfer to a serving platter or individual plates. Top with shrimp and serve immediately.

Serves 4

Shao Hsing is rice wine, and is available in most liquor stores. Saki can be substituted.

Three-Cheese Crab Quesadillas

*These appetizing little treats are filling and satisfying as a main entrée.
Try serving with a salad or Sesame Green Beans (109)*

*They also make wonderful hors d'oeuvres
For anything from formal cocktail parties to backyard barbecues!*

1-1/2 cups Pacific whitefish (imitation crabmeat), chopped
1 cup shredded Monterey Jack cheese (divided)
1/2 cup shredded mozzarella cheese
1/2 cup shredded cheddar cheese
12-ounce jar chile sauce (divided)

10 scallions with green tops, thinly sliced (divided)
2 cloves garlic, minced
8 8" flour tortillas
About 1/4 cup butter (divided)

Combine whitefish, 1/2 cup Monterey Jack cheese, the mozzarella cheese, cheddar cheese, 1/2 cup chile sauce, 5 scallions, and garlic in medium bowl. Mix well.

Place equal amounts of the cheese mixture on each of 4 tortillas, spreading to within 1/2" of tortilla edges. Top with remaining tortillas, lightly pressing together with your fingers.

Place a large skillet over medium heat and melt about 2 teaspoons of butter. Add one quesadilla and cook for about 2 minutes on each side or until crisp and golden brown on the outside and cheese has begun to melt on the inside. Repeat with remaining quesadillas, using additional butter as needed.

Meanwhile, in a small skillet, sauté remaining scallions in about a teaspoon of butter until soft.

Cut each quesadilla into 4 wedges (*8 wedges for hors d'oeuvres*), sprinkle with remaining Jack cheese and sautéed scallions.

Serve with remaining chile sauce.

Serves 4

Pepper-Powered Poultry

- *Chicken Enchiladas*

- *Enchiladas Sauce*

- *Chicken Fajitas*

- *Fried Chicken Chimichangas*

- *Cilantro Turkey Burgers with Chipotle Chile Mayonnaise*

- *Chipotle Mayonnaise*

- *Southwestern Chicken Stew*

- *Texas Turkey Hash and Eggs*

- *Turkey Mole'*

Chicken Enchiladas

Ole!!! Savour the flavour of this snappy casserole!

Enchilada Sauce (*Recipe below*)
2 cups cooked, finely diced chicken breast
1 large onion, finely chopped
2 tablespoons finely chopped cilantro
2 cups shredded Monterey Jack cheese
    (divided)

10 small or 5 large flour tortillas
Suggested Condiments: Sour cream, **Cinco De Mayo Guacamole** (25), shredded lettuce, and tomato wedges

Prepare Enchilada Sauce.

Preheat oven to 350 degrees.

While Enchilada Sauce is cooking, combine chicken, onion, cilantro, and 1 cup of cheese. Divide evenly and spread over tortillas. Roll up each tortilla tightly (jellyroll fashion) and place seam-side-down in a 9 x 13" baking pan.

Pour sauce over enchiladas and sprinkle with remaining cheese.

Bake for 35 to 40 minutes.

Serve with sour cream, guacamole, lettuce, and tomatoes.

Serves 5

Enchilada Sauce:

1 medium onion, chopped fine
2 cloves garlic, minced
2 tablespoons vegetable oil
15-ounce can tomato sauce
1 cup chicken broth

1 teaspoon Chili Powder (24)
1 teaspoon cumin powder
1/8 teaspoon cayenne pepper
1 teaspoon hot sauce

In a saucepan, sauté onion and garlic in oil until onion is translucent. Add remaining ingredients and simmer, uncovered, for 20 minutes, stirring occasionally.

Chicken Fajitas

(Pronounced fuh-HEET-uhs)

Sitting around the table with family or friends can be more fun than ever when you serve fajitas!
(You can easily substitute chicken with whole shrimp or strips of beef or pork.)

4 boneless, skinless chicken breast halves, washed, patted dry, and cut into 1/4" strips
8 6" flour tortillas
1-1/2 teaspoons fajita seasoning mix
1/8 cup vegetable oil (divided)
2 medium green bell peppers , sliced in 1/4" strips
2 medium red bell peppers , sliced in 1/4" strips

*1 large onion, sliced in 1/4" slices
Suggested Accompaniments:
       Cinco De Mayo Guacamole (25)
       Salsa Verde (30)
       Shredded lettuce
       Chopped tomatoes
       Sliced black olives
       Sour cream

Sprinkle chicken strips with fajita seasoning. Refrigerate for one hour.

Meanwhile, prepare accompaniments and place in individual bowls or arrange in lettuce "cups" on a platter.

Just before it's time to start cooking the fajitas, wrap tortillas in foil and warm in a 350-degree oven for 5 to 7 minutes.

Heat a cast iron skillet until very hot. Add half the oil. Add chicken strips to skillet, keeping heat medium high, and stirring constantly for about 2 minutes. Transfer to a heated platter.

Add remaining oil to skillet. When hot, add peppers and onion. Cook for 2 minutes, stirring.

Return chicken to pan and continue cooking over medium high heat and stirring occasionally until chicken is cooked through and vegetables are cooked but still slightly crisp (about 3 minutes).

Place sizzling skillet on a trivet and invite all to help themselves by transferring fajita mixture to tortillas and topping with accompaniments before folding or rolling up!

Serves 4

* Slicing Onions:

- ♦ *Using a cutting board, slice off both ends of the onion.*

- ♦ *Place one of the flat ends of the onion onto the board and slice in half, along the axis.*

- ♦ *Peel off the dry, papery layers.*

- ♦ *Place the onion halves onto the cutting board (flat-side-down) and then proceed to slice as thin as you need.*

- ♦ ***Keep your fingertips:*** *You may want to keep your fingertips and thumb tucked slightly inward to prevent cutting yourself.*

Fried Chicken Chimichangas

If your tortillas are not soft and pliable, place 2 or 3 at a time in a well-rung, damp dishtowel and put in a warm oven for 1 minute. The steam will make them very manageable for rolling.

1 clove garlic, minced
1 medium onion, diced
2 tomatoes, diced
1/2 teaspoon ground cumin
1 tablespoon extra-virgin olive oil
2 cups diced cooked chicken
4-ounce can mild green chilies, drained

1 teaspoon salt
1 cup Monterey Jack cheese, shredded
8 10" flour tortillas
Vegetable oil for frying
Suggested Condiments: **Vegetable Salsa** (35),
Cinco De Mayo Guacamole (25), sour cream,
   shredded lettuce, and diced tomatoes

Combine garlic, onion, tomatoes, and cumin in a bowl.

Heat olive oil in a frying pan. Add tomato mixture and sauté over medium heat for 3 minutes. Lower heat and simmer for 5 more minutes.

Add chicken, chilies, and salt. Stir well. Raise temperature to boiling and stir until no trace of liquid appears (about 5 minutes). Remove pan from heat. Cool.

Stir cheese into cooled chicken mixture.

Place equal portions of chicken mixture in the center of each tortilla. Fold tortillas in half to cover filling and then fold in the two sides envelope fashion and roll up. Fasten with wooden picks if necessary.

Heat 1" of vegetable oil in a skillet until the temperature reaches 350 degrees. Place chimichangas seam-side-down in the heated oil and fry about 1-1/2 minutes. Turn and continue frying an additional 1-1/2 minute or until golden brown.

Using a large slotted spoon, transfer chimichangas to a layer of paper towels to drain and then to a heated platter.

Serve with salsa, guacamole, sour cream, lettuce, and tomatoes.

Serves 4 to 8

Cilantro Turkey Burgers with Chipotle Chile Mayonnaise

The rich flavour of fresh cilantro enhances this low-fat burger.
Of course, the addition of the Chipotle Chile Mayonnaise cancels out any prospect of low fat...
but it's well worth it...so ENJOY!

Chipotle Mayonnaise *(Recipe next page)*
1-1/2 pounds ground turkey
1 cup fresh cilantro leaves, finely chopped
1/4 cup finely chopped onion
4 cloves minced garlic
1/2 teaspoon salt

1 egg, beaten
1/2 cup breadcrumbs
1 tablespoon olive oil
4 hard rolls
Suggested Condiments: Sliced onion and
    lettuce

Prepare Chipotle Mayonnaise.

Combine turkey, cilantro, onion, garlic, salt, egg, and breadcrumbs in a bowl. Shape into four patties.

Coat a large frying pan with oil and heat over medium high heat. Fry burgers for 5 minutes on each side or until nicely browned and meat thermometer inserted in center registers 160 degrees.

Serve on hard rolls slathered with Chipotle Chile Mayonnaise and topped with sliced onion and lettuce.

Serves 4

Chipotle Mayonnaise:

1 cup mayonnaise	1 tablespoon fresh lime juice
1 tablespoon canned chipotle chilies, drained	1/2 teaspoon lime zest
1 clove garlic, minced	1 tablespoon minced scallions

Blend all ingredients in a small bowl. Cover and refrigerate until ready to use.

Chipotle (pronounced chih-POHT-lay) (smoked jalapeño) is medium-hot pepper with a deep, smoky sweet flavour. It has a wrinkled, dark brown skin when dried and can also be found pickled or packed in canned adobo (pronounced ah-DOH-boh) sauce. Chipotles are often added to stews and sauces and the pickled variety are normally eaten as an appetizer or are served with sandwiches.

Adobo is a dark-red, rather piquant sauce made from ground chilies, herbs, and vinegar. It is used as a marinade as well as a serving sauce. (See Adobo Sauce, Page 103.)

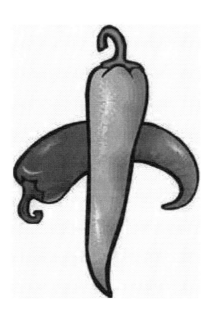

Southwestern Chicken Stew

Phenomenal flavour…this is a chicken version of chili with beans!

2 pounds skinless, boneless chicken thighs, trimmed of all fat and cut in 1" cubes
1/4 cup oil
1 large onion, cut up
4 large cloves garlic, slivered
1/2 cup chopped fresh cilantro
1/2 teaspoon ground hot red chile pepper
1/2 teaspoon paprika
1 teaspoon dried oregano flakes

1 teaspoon cumin
1-pound, 12-ounce can crushed tomatoes
1-pound can black beans, drained
1-pound can cannellini beans (white kidney beans), drained
1-pound can red kidney beans, drained
1 cup shredded asadero/queso blanco/Jack cheese blend (*or* Monterey Jack)

Heat oil in a large, heavy skillet. Add chicken, onion, and garlic. Sauté over medium-high heat, stirring occasionally, until brown.

Meanwhile, in a medium-sized bowl, combine cilantro, hot chile pepper, paprika, oregano, cumin, and crushed tomatoes. Add to chicken with beans and stir well.

Cover and simmer for 30 minutes.

Serve with cheese.

Serves 8

Texas Turkey Hash and Eggs

Left over turkey?
This is a Sunday morning eye-opener that your family will love!

3 tablespoons vegetable oil
1 large onion, chopped
2 jalapeño peppers (seeds and ribs removed),
   finely chopped
3 cups shredded potatoes (skin-on)
1-1/2 cups finely diced, cooked turkey
1 cup canned corn, drained

3/4 cup chicken bouillon
1 teaspoon salt
1/2 teaspoon ground cumin
1/2 teaspoon ground black pepper
4 eggs
Hot sauce *(for serving)*

Pour oil into a very large, *ovenproof* skillet. Add onion and jalapeños and sauté for 3 minutes or until tender.

Add potatoes, turkey, and corn. Combine bouillon with salt, cumin, and black pepper and add to hash. Stir to blend.

Cook over medium heat for about 30 minutes, or until hash is nicely browned, occasionally turning mixture with a spatula during cooking.

Separate hash into four portions. Shape each portion into a round mound and form a well in the center of each with the back of a spoon. Drop an egg into each well. Cover skillet and simmer over medium to low heat for two minutes. Place under the broiler for about 30 to 60 seconds, or until eggs are done.

Remove each portion to serving dishes with a spatula and serve immediately with hot sauce on the side.

Serves 4

Turkey Mole'

Mole' is a classic sauce that is as Mexican as turkey is American!

And its versatility makes it a great companion to anything –
poultry, beef, pork, seafood, and vegetables!
So, while you're at it, whip up an extra batch for another meal!

6 dried pasilla chilies
1 medium onion, finely chopped
3 tablespoons water
1 large tomato (peeled and chopped)
1/4 cup cilantro, chopped
2 tablespoons unsalted smooth peanut butter
2 tablespoons raisins, chopped
1 ounce unsweetened chocolate, finely chopped
1 clove garlic, minced
1/2 teaspoon salt
1/2 teaspoon sugar

1/2 teaspoon ground cinnamon
1/2 teaspoon whole cloves
1/2 teaspoon whole allspice
1-3/4 cups chicken stock
2 pounds turkey breast (cut in 1/2 x 3"
   strips)
Salt *(to sprinkle turkey)*
3 tablespoons vegetable oil (use as needed)
Suggested Accompaniments: Warm tortillas,
   sour cream, shredded Monterrey Jack
   cheese

Pull the stems off the chilies and shake out the seeds. Tear into small pieces, put into a bowl, and cover with boiling water. Soak for 30 minutes. Drain *(save liquid for seasoning another dish!)*.

Place chilies, onion, and water in a large, nonstick skillet over medium-low heat. Cover and cook until soft (about 8 minutes), stirring occasionally.

Add next 11 ingredients and stir to combine. Continue to cook over low heat for about 10 minutes.

Bring chicken stock to boil in small saucepan. Gradually stir stock into chile mixture. Simmer uncovered until the sauce thickens, stirring occasionally (about 45 to 50 minutes).

Just before mole' is done, lightly sprinkle turkey with salt. Add some of the oil to a large, nonstick skillet and place over medium-high heat. Add turkey and cook until light golden and no longer pink in the center (about 3 minutes per side). (You may have to do this in batches, adding more oil as needed.)

Preheat oven to 350 degrees.

Transfer turkey to an ovenproof dish.

Whirl mole' in a blender until smooth and pour over turkey. Cover and place in oven for about 15 minutes.

Serve with warm tortillas, sour cream, and shredded Jack.

Serves 4 to 6

Mole' (pronounced MOH-lea) is derived from the Aztec word for sauce and is the national dish of Mexico. Customarily, making mole' is an involved process combining tomatillos or tomatoes with several varieties of chilies, sesame or pumpkinseeds, and Mexican chocolate. And, surprisingly to many Americans who think of mole' as a "chocolate sauce", there is comparatively very little chocolate in the recipe. The chocolate is used mainly to provide a deep, rich colour to the sauce.

ALL BEEFED-UP

- ❑ *Beef Burritos*
- ❑ *Beef Empanadas*
- ❑ *Chili in a Bread Bowl*
- ❑ *Beef Tacos*
- ❑ *Mexican Lasagna*
- ❑ *Pasta with Mexican Beef Sauce*
- ❑ *Quick Tex-Mex Beef and Corn*
- ❑ *Stuffed Mushroom Cheese Burgers*
- ❑ *Red Beans and Rice*
- ❑ *Taco Pizza*
- ❑ *Tamale Pie*
- ❑ *Texas Chili for a Crowd*
- ❑ *Three-Chile Chili*

Beef Burritos

Muy delicioso y fácil de hacer!
(Very delicious and easy to make!)
Or…as the grandchildren say…"AWESOME!!!"

1 small onion, chopped
1/4 cup water
1 pound lean ground beef
3 cups prepared salsa (mild, medium, or hot)
   (divided)

1-1/2 cup mild shredded cheddar cheese
   (divided)
4 large or 8 small flour tortillas (plain or
   jalapeño flavoured)
Suggested Condiments: **Cinco De Mayo**
   Guacamole (25) and sour cream

Preheat oven to 375 degrees.

In a non-stick frying pan, boil onion in water until onion is soft and liquid has evaporated.

Add ground beef and sauté over medium-high heat, stirring occasionally, until meat is well browned. Drain off and discard fat.

Stir in 1-1/2 cups of salsa and simmer for 5 minutes, stirring occasionally.

Remove from heat and let stand for about 15 minutes to cool.

Add 1 cup cheddar cheese and stir well to blend.

Spread equal amounts of beef mixture over tortillas. Roll and place seam-side-down in an 11 x 14" baking dish.

Pour remaining salsa over burritos and sprinkle with remaining cheese.

Bake for 20 minutes.

Serve with guacamole and sour cream.

Serves 4

Beef Empanadas

Empanadas are baked or fried Mexican turnovers filled with sweet or savoury fillings.

*This beef version of the empanada is a delightful main dish pastry
...and the crust will melt in your mouth!*

Filling:

2 tablespoons butter
1/2 cup chopped onion
1 pound ground round
2 large tomatoes, chopped
3-ounce can chopped green chilies, drained
Bay leaf
1/4 teaspoon salt

1/4 cup finely chopped black olives
Empanada Pastry *(Recipe next page)*
1 egg yolk and 1 tablespoon water, beaten
  together
Suggested Condiments: **Salsa Verde** (30), and
  sour cream
Suggested Accompaniment: **Frijoles Refritos**
  (107)

In a medium-size fry pan, sauté onion in butter until tender. Add beef and brown lightly.

Add tomatoes, green chilies, bay leaf, and salt. Simmer uncovered, stirring occasionally, 30 to 35 minutes or until most of the liquid has evaporated.

Remove pan from heat, discard bay leaf, and stir in olives. Cool until lukewarm.

Meanwhile, prepare pastry.

Preheat oven to 400 degrees.

Divide pastry into 8 pieces. On a lightly floured surface, roll each piece into a 7" round. Place about 3 tablespoons of filling on one half of each round and fold pastry over filling.

Press edges together and flute with fingers to seal. Pierce the top of each empanada with a fork to vent. Brush with egg wash.

Place empanadas on an ungreased, non-stick baking sheet.

Bake for 20 to 25 minutes or until golden brown.

Serve hot...and enjoy!

Serves 4

Empanada Pastry:

1-1/2 cups flour   1/2 cup shortening
1/4 teaspoon salt   4-1/2 tablespoons ice water

In a medium bowl, combine flour and salt. With a pastry blender, cut in shortening until mixture resembles coarse crumbs. Sprinkle with ice water and stir with fork until mixture holds together. Shape into a ball.

Chili in a Bread Bowl

Mis amigos, usted adorará esto!
(My friends, you will love this!)

Surrounding the Chili "Bowl" with brightly coloured raw vegetables provides both eye appeal and crisp munching to accompany this spicy and delicious variation of chili!

2 pounds lean ground beef
2 tablespoons Chili Powder (24)
1 teaspoon hot sauce
2 tablespoons olive oil
2 medium onions, chopped
1 medium green bell pepper, chopped
1 habañero or Scotch bonnet pepper (seeds and ribs removed), finely diced
2-pound can diced tomatoes

1-pound can kidney beans, drained and rinsed
1-pound can whole kernel corn, drained
1 large round loaf sourdough, pumpernickel, or rye bread
1 cup shredded Monterey Jack cheese
Suggested Accompaniments: Assorted Raw Vegetables

In a large skillet, sauté beef, stirring occasionally, until brown. Drain off excess fat.

Add chili powder and hot sauce. Stir to blend. Transfer to a bowl and set aside.

Add oil to pan with onions and peppers. Sauté for about five minutes, stirring occasionally. Add beef, tomatoes, kidney beans, and corn. Bring to a boil and stir. Reduce heat, cover, and simmer for about 20 minutes.

Meanwhile, prepare bread bowl: Using a serrated knife, take a thin slice off the bottom of the bread so that it will set well on a plate. Slice off about an inch from the top of the bread. Carve out the center to form a bowl, leaving about 1" of bread around the inside. *(Cut carved-out bread into small cubes to dry for breadcrumbs or croutons for another use.)*

Place bread bowl on a round platter and fill with chili. Top with shredded cheese. Serve immediately with raw veggies...*and be sure to "clean up your 'bowl'"!*

Serves 6

Habañero and Scotch bonnet peppers are **extremely** *hot! If your tolerance for heat is mediocre, try substituting a milder version, such as poblano or Hungarian wax.*

Beef Tacos

*Children **LOVE** tacos!*

This is a quick fix for the fast-paced life of the typical American family.

1 pound lean ground beef
14-1/2 ounce can peeled and chopped
   tomatoes with liquid
1 medium green bell pepper, seeded and
   finely chopped
1 envelope onion soup mix
2 teaspoons Chili Powder (24)

2 or 3 drops hot pepper sauce
4 taco shells
Suggested Toppings: Shredded Monterey Jack,
   shredded lettuce, chopped tomatoes,
   sliced pitted black olives, diced onion, sour
   cream, and taco sauce or salsa

In a medium skillet, brown ground beef over medium-high heat. Drain and discard fat.

Stir in tomatoes, green pepper, onion soup mix, chili powder, and hot pepper sauce. Bring to a boil. Reduce heat and simmer (uncovered) for 15 minutes.

Serve in taco shells with assorted toppings.

Serves 4

Mexican Lasagna

There are just times, mis amigos, when you just HAVE to let go...and forget the calories!

1 pound ground round
12-ounce jar chunky salsa (mild or medium) (divided)
9 10" corn tortillas
1-pound can refried beans (divided) (or **Frijoles Refritos** 107)

1 cup ricotta (divided)
2-1/4 cups shredded Mexican-style four-cheese blend (divided)
Suggested Accompaniments: Chopped tomatoes and scallions

Preheat oven to 400 degrees.

Mist a large skillet with cooking spray and place over medium-high heat. Add ground beef and brown, stirring occasionally, until cooked through (about 5 minutes). Drain off and discard any fat.

Stir 1/2 cup of salsa into the beef. Set aside.

Spread half of the remaining salsa in the bottom of a 10" pie pan. Top with 3 tortillas. Spread half the beans over the tortillas, then half of the meat mixture, and 1/2 cup of ricotta. Sprinkle with 1 cup of the cheese blend.

Top with 3 more tortillas and repeat the bean/meat/ricotta/cheese blend layers, ending with the remaining tortillas.

Top with remaining salsa and cheese blend.

Cover pie pan loosely with aluminum foil.

Bake until cheese has melted and the lasagna is hot throughout (about 15 minutes). Remove from oven. Let rest for 5 minutes before cutting into wedges.

Serve with chopped tomatoes and scallions.

Serves 4 to 6

Pasta with Mexican Beef Sauce

The wagon wheel pasta gives this dish a chuck wagon look...just for fun!

2 teaspoons vegetable oil
1 cup chopped onions
1 pound lean ground beef
1/2 teaspoon ground cumin
1 teaspoon Chili Powder(24)
1 teaspoon minced garlic
1 teaspoon salt

6 cups chopped fresh ripe tomatoes
1 pound wagon wheel pasta, cooked
   according to package directions
1 cup shredded pepper Jack cheese
Suggested Accompaniments: Crushed
   tortilla chips and sliced green onions

Heat oil in large skillet over medium-high heat. Add onions and cook until softened (about 5 minutes). Remove from pan.

Add ground beef to skillet and brown well. Drain off and discard fat.

Add softened onion, cumin, chili powder, garlic, and salt. Stir well.

Add tomatoes and bring to a boil, stirring. Reduce heat and simmer (uncovered) for about 10 minutes.

Meanwhile, begin cooking pasta.

Drain pasta and transfer to a serving bowl.

Add sauce to pasta and fold in cheese.

Serve with crushed tortilla chips and sliced green onions.

Serves 4

Quick Tex-Mex Beef and Corn

Get home from work late? ... Ningún problema!
Just add a salad and...lickety-split...you're done!

1 pound ground beef, browned (drain off and discard fat)

1-pound can whole kernel corn, drained

1 cup prepared salsa (mild or medium)

1/2 cup shredded Jack cheese

Combine beef with corn and salsa. Turn into a 1-quart casserole dish. Sprinkle with cheese.

Bake in a 350-degree oven for 30 to 35 minutes.

Serves 4

Stuffed Mushroom Cheese Burgers

*These burgers are so flavourful and juicy
you probably won't need any condiments.*

But feel free to add lettuce, tomato, and mayo if you like!

1-1/2 cups shredded pepper Jack cheese
1/3 cup chopped black olives
1-3/4 pounds lean ground beef
1/4 cup finely chopped onion
1/2 cup finely chopped fresh mushrooms

2 tablespoons Worcestershire Sauce
1/2 teaspoon ground black pepper
4 deli-size hamburger buns
Melted butter
Condiment: **Hot sauce**

Lightly oil a perforated barbecue grid and preheat at medium-hot temperature.

In a medium bowl, combine cheese and olives. Divide the mixture into 4 portions. Shape into balls and slightly flatten.

Mix ground beef with onion, mushrooms, Worcestershire, and pepper. Shape into 8 thin patties.

Top each of four patties with one portion of the cheese and olive mixture. Cover with remaining patties and seal edges to enclose cheese.

Grill patties on a covered grill for 5 or 6 minutes on each side, or until done.

About 3 minutes before burgers are done, split buns, brush with melted butter, and place (cut-side down) on grill to heat through.

Using a spatula, transfer burgers to heated buns. Serve with hot sauce on the side and *enjoy!*

Serves 4

Red Beans and Rice

This dish stands proudly as a hearty entrée.
Serve with a salad and crusty bread!

1-1/2 pound lean ground beef
2 15-ounce cans red kidney beans, drained
1-pound jar picante sauce
2 cups water
1 cup uncooked white rice

1/2 cup chopped green bell pepper
1-1/2 teaspoons paprika
1 tablespoon Chili Powder (24)
1/2 teaspoon crushed red pepper flakes
8 ounces sharp cheddar cheese, shredded

Place ground beef in a large skillet over medium-high heat. Sauté for 10 minutes, stirring. When beef has browned, transfer to a large pot, discarding any fat.

Add kidney beans, picante sauce, water, rice, green pepper, paprika, chili powder, and red pepper flakes. Turn up heat and bring mixture to a boil, stirring. Reduce heat, cover, and simmer for 20 minutes.

Add additional water if necessary. Stir in cheese and simmer for 10 more minutes.

Stir lightly with a fork. Transfer to a serving bowl and serve!

Serves 5

Taco Pizza

Using refrigerated bread dough makes this spicy pizza a snap!

1 pound ground beef
1 cup tomato sauce
1/4 cup water
1-1/4-ounce package taco seasoning mix
13-ounce tube refrigerated Italian bread dough
8 ounces shredded Monterrey Jack cheese

1/4 cup canned jalapeño peppers (sliced and drained)
1/2 cup shredded lettuce
1/2 cup diced tomato
1/4 cup sliced black olives, drained
Condiment: Sour cream

Brown beef in a skillet. Drain off and discard fat. Add tomato sauce, water, and seasoning mix. Stir to blend. Simmer for 5 minutes.

Grease a 12" pizza pan and roll or stretch the dough to cover the surface, pressing together to seal any tears. Prick dough with a fork every few inches and bake at 375 degrees for 12 minutes.

Spread beef mixture over the crust and top with shredded cheese and jalapeño peppers. Continue baking for 8 to 10 minutes, or until cheese is melted.

Top with lettuce, tomatoes, and olives. Cut into wedges and serve with sour cream.

Serves 4

Tamale Pie

Try it - you'll like it!

Polenta *(Recipe below)*
1 medium onion, chopped
1 jalapeño pepper (seeds and ribs removed), finely chopped
1 clove garlic, minced
3 teaspoons extra virgin olive oil
1 pound lean ground beef
6-ounce can tomato paste mixed with 1 can water

1 teaspoon hot sauce
1-pound can whole kernel corn, drained
1-pound can pitted black olives, drained and sliced
1 teaspoon salt
1/4 teaspoon pepper
1 teaspoon Chili Powder (24)
1/4 teaspoon paprika
1/2 cup shredded Jack cheese
Paprika *(for sprinkling)*

Prepare polenta. Remove from heat and cover.

In a large skillet, sauté onion, jalapeño pepper, and garlic in oil until onion begins to brown. Remove from pan and set aside.

Add beef to skillet and brown well over medium-high heat. Drain off and discard fat.

Return sautéed onion/pepper/garlic to pan. Add tomato paste and water, hot sauce, corn, olives, salt, pepper, chili powder, and paprika. Bring to a boil, stirring. Reduce heat and simmer (uncovered) for about 10 minutes.

Spread 1/2 of the polenta on the bottom of a deep 9"-round pie dish. Cover with beef mixture. Spread remaining cornmeal over top. Sprinkle with shredded Jack and paprika.

Bake for 40 to 45 minutes at 375 degrees.

Slice into wedges and serve!

Serves 6

Polenta

4 cups water (divided)
1 teaspoon salt

1 cup yellow cornmeal

In a heavy pot, bring 3 cups of water and the salt to a boil.

Meanwhile, mix cornmeal into 1 cup of cold water. Slowly add to boiling water, stirring constantly. Cook until thickened, stirring frequently. Cover and cook over low heat for about 20 minutes, stirring occasionally and adding additional water if needed. The polenta is done when the mixture begins to pull away from the sides of the pot.

Texas Chili for a Crowd

A big bowl o' red...
made the way Texans intended it to be ... no beans!
Savoury and tender chunks of beef in a delicious tomato-based sauce!

10 pounds boneless chuck roast
1/2 cup vegetable oil (more if needed)
2 large onions, chopped
8 green bell peppers, finely chopped
3 Anaheim chilies (seeds and ribs
  removed), finely chopped
15 garlic cloves, minced

3 pounds ripe tomatoes, cut up
18 ounces tomato paste mixed with 1 cup water
1/8 cup Chili Powder (24)
2 tablespoons sugar
1 tablespoon salt
1 tablespoon oregano flakes
1 teaspoon ground black pepper

Trim beef of all fat and cut into 1/2" cubes. Add a few tablespoons of oil to a heavy pot. Sear a batch of beef over high heat. Remove to a bowl. Repeat until all beef has been seared.

Add onions, peppers, and garlic to drippings in pan. Cook over medium heat for 10 minutes, stirring occasionally. (Add additional oil if necessary.)

Return the meat to the pot. Add tomatoes, tomato paste and water, chili powder, sugar, salt, oregano, and pepper. Stir well. Bring to a boil. Cover, reduce heat, and simmer for 1 hour or until meat is tender.

Serves 12

Three-Chile Chili

The rich, hearty sauce in this chili can be attributed to the chile pepper and beer puree that is added to the beef for a slow, aromatic simmer.

Serve with fresh hard rolls to sop up the gravy and add a salad to make this meal complete.

Incredibly fantastic!

5 pounds boneless beef chuck roast
3 Jalapeño chile peppers (seeds and ribs removed), cut up
3 Hungarian wax chile peppers (seeds and ribs removed), cut up
3 Anaheim chile peppers (seeds and ribs removed), cut up
16 ounces beer

3 tablespoons vegetable oil (divided)
1 large onion, coarsely chopped
6 large cloves garlic, minced
2 cups beef broth
1/2 teaspoon ground cumin
1 tablespoon oregano flakes
1 teaspoon sugar
2 teaspoons salt

Trim beef of fat and cut into 1/2" cubes. Set aside.

Place chile peppers in a large saucepan with beer. Bring to a boil, reduce heat, and simmer for 30 minutes.

Meanwhile, heat 1 tablespoon of the oil in a large skillet, and sauté onion for 5 minutes. Add garlic and sauté an additional minute or two. Remove onions and garlic from heat and set aside.

Add a tablespoon of oil to skillet. Sear half of the beef over high heat, stirring frequently. Remove from pan. Repeat with remaining beef and oil.

Pour cooked chilies and liquid to a blender or food processor and puree.

Transfer beef, onion and garlic, chile puree, broth, cumin, oregano, sugar, and salt to a large, heavy pot. Stir. Bring to a boil, cover, reduce heat, and simmer for 1 hour or until meat is very tender.

Serves 6

Pork with a Punch

❏   ***BJ's Jalapeño Pepper Sauce with Sausage over Pasta***

❏   ***Mexican Pork Stew***

❏   ***Spare Ribs with Chipotle Honey Barbecue Sauce***

❏   ***Adobo Sauce***

❏   ***Shredded Pork Wraps***

BJ's Jalapeño Pepper Sauce with Sausage over Pasta

Jumpin' Jalapeños! This is one zesty and satisfying meal!
Just add some crusty bread and a salad!

8 links hot sausage, cut up in 1" pieces
1 tablespoon extra-virgin olive oil
1 cup chopped onion
4 jalapeños chilies (seeds and ribs removed),
   chopped
1/2 cup chopped cilantro

3 pounds ripe tomatoes, diced
2 teaspoons oregano flakes
1/2 teaspoon cumin
1 teaspoon salt
1 pound pasta, cooked al dente
1 cup shredded Colby cheese

Cook sausage in a heavy skillet until nicely browned and thoroughly cooked. Drain off and discard all fat.

Add oil, onion, jalapeños, and cilantro to skillet. Sauté until onions are brown.

Meanwhile, combine tomatoes, oregano, cumin, and salt in a heavy pot. Stir until mixture comes to a boil. Add sausage mixture. Stir to blend. Cover pot, reduce heat, and simmer for 1 hour, stirring occasionally.

Begin cooking pasta shortly before sauce is done. Drain.

Transfer pasta into a serving bowl. Cover with sausage sauce. Sprinkle with cheese and serve!

Serves 4 to 6

Mexican Pork Stew

*This dish may take a little extra time to prepare, but it's **worth** it!*
You will love the tender, rich, and flavourful end result.

*...AND...any leftovers (if there **are** any) can be divvied up into individual casseroles, frozen, and reheated for homemade TV dinners!*

1-1/2 pounds tomatillos (husks removed and discarded)
4 tablespoons extra-virgin olive oil (divided)
3 pounds pork shoulder, cut into 1" cubes
1 large white onion, chopped
3 garlic cloves, minced
3 Hungarian wax peppers (stems and seeds removed), chopped
1 teaspoon dried oregano
1/2 teaspoon ground cumin
3 cups chicken broth

Polenta (95)
1/4 cup flour mixed with 1/2 cup water
1-pound can black beans, drained
1-pound can corn, drained
1/2 cup chopped fresh cilantro
Suggested Accompaniments:
   2 peeled and sliced avocados
   3/4 cup chopped white onion
   3/4 cup sour cream
   3 Hungarian wax peppers (stems and seeds removed), finely chopped

Heat broiler.

Arrange tomatillos in a large baking pan and broil 6" from heat until lightly charred, turning occasionally. Cut in quarters and set aside.

Heat 1 tablespoon of oil in a heavy Dutch oven. Sear pork in 3 batches, using additional oil as needed. Transfer to a bowl.

Add remaining oil, onion, garlic, 3 wax peppers, oregano, and cumin to the pot. Cook over moderate heat until onion is soft.

Add tomatillos, broth, and browned pork to pot. Bring to a boil. Stir, cover pot, reduce heat, and simmer for about 1 hour (or until pork is tender).

Meanwhile, prepare polenta and keep warm.

Gradually stir flour mixture into stew. Add beans, corn, and cilantro. Simmer, *uncovered*, stirring occasionally, until slightly thickened (about 10 minutes).

Serve over Polenta with bowls of suggested accompaniments on the side!

Unbelievably delicious !!!

Serves 6

Spare Ribs with Chipotle Honey Barbecue Sauce

...You will love the subtle, smoky flavour that the chipotle peppers impart...

These melt-in-your mouth, juicy, tender, and delicious ribs
are great for winter suppers or summer patio parties.
Serve with a simple salad and Corn with Chile Lime Butter (106) or baked potatoes!

2 tablespoons Adobo Sauce *(Recipe*
  next page)
4 2-pound slabs of pork ribs
1 teaspoon salt (divided)
1 teaspoon garlic powder
1/2 teaspoon black pepper

2 bay leaves
2 tablespoons canola oil
1 medium onion, finely diced
1 cup ketchup
1/4 cup cider vinegar
1/4 cup honey

Prepare Adobo Sauce.

Bring a large pot of water to a boil. Add spare ribs, 1/2 teaspoon of salt, garlic powder, black pepper, and bay leaves. Cover, reduce heat and simmer for 1 hour or until ribs are tender.

Meanwhile, heat oil in a saucepan over medium heat. Add onion and cook, stirring occasionally, until the onion softens and begins to brown (about 10 minutes).

Add the ketchup, vinegar, honey, adobo sauce, and remaining salt to onions. Stir to combine. Reduce the heat to low and cook, uncovered, for 15 minutes. Remove the pan from the heat.

Preheat the grill at medium setting (or set oven temperature to 350 degrees).

Remove ribs from broth, discard bay leaves, and place in a baking pan. Coat the ribs with 2/3 of the sauce. (Reserve remaining 1/3 for serving.)

Either place ribs directly on the barbecue grill and heat for 15 minutes, turning once; or place the baking pan into the oven for 20 minutes.

Transfer to a serving platter. Serve remaining sauce on the side.

Serves 6 to 8

Adobo Sauce

10 whole chipotle peppers (smoked and dried jalapeños) (stems and seeds removed), cut up
1/3 cup onion, diced
5 tablespoons cider vinegar
2 cloves garlic, sliced

1/4 cup catsup
3 cups water
1/4 teaspoon cumin
1/2 teaspoon oregano flakes
1/2 teaspoon salt

Put all ingredients in a medium-sized saucepot. Bring to a boil. Cover, reduce to low heat, and simmer for about 2 hours or until the chilies are very soft and the liquid has been reduced to 1 cup.

Process in a blender until sauce is smooth.

Makes 1 Cup

Freeze excess in ice cube trays. When frozen, transfer to a freezer bag until ready to use.

Shredded Pork Wraps

... A takeoff on pulled pork sandwiches ....

*This version cooks the pork slowly in the oven.
The meat simmers in its own juices, capturing the full flavour of the rub.
And the sauce is spicy and delicious!*

Freeze any leftovers for a quick meal later on...

7 tablespoons paprika
1 teaspoon cayenne pepper
4 teaspoons salt
4 teaspoons black pepper
4 teaspoons onion powder
4 teaspoons garlic powder
2 teaspoons cumin

10-pound pork loin roast
12 10" flour tortillas
Accompaniments:
   2 cups shredded Colby cheese
   3 sliced ripe tomatoes
   2 cups shredded lettuce
   3 pitted, peeled, and sliced avocados

Mix spices together in a small bowl. Give the outside of the meat a generous rub with the spice blend.

Place meat in a covered roasting pan and put in a 275-degree oven.

Roast for 10 hours, turning meat every two hours.

Remove roast from oven. Cool for 1 hour.

Meanwhile, skim and discard fat from the pan drippings. Strain. Keep sauce warm to serve with wraps.

When meat is cool enough to handle, remove and discard the bone and all trace of fat. Pull meat into strips and transfer to a serving platter.

Serve in tortillas with sauce and suggested accompaniments.

Serves 12

Vegetables and Rice for Chile Heads

- ❑ *Corn with Chile Lime Butter*

- ❑ *Chile Paste*

- ❑ *Frijoles Refritos*

- ❑ *Roasted Mexican-Style Vegetables*

- ❑ *Sesame Green Beans*

- ❑ *Red Rice*

- ❑ *Spanish Rice*

Corn with Chile Lime Butter

*Grilling corn on the cob is a very popular way to serve this summer-time treat ...
but adding the chile lime butter adds a whole new dimension to flavourful outdoor cooking!*

6 ears fresh corn (husks on)
1/4 pound unsalted butter, softened
1 tablespoon minced garlic
Juice of 1 lime
2 tablespoons chopped cilantro

2 tablespoons canned chile paste *(or make your own!...instructions below)*
1/2 teaspoon ground cumin
Salt and pepper to taste

Strip back corn husks as you would peel a banana. Remove the silk and gather husks so that you have a "handle" at one end. Tie with a string. Soak the ears (and husks) in cold water for 30 minutes.

Preheat the grill to medium heat.

Combine butter, garlic, lime juice, cilantro, chile paste, and cumin in a small pan. Add salt and pepper as desired. Heat to melt and set aside.

Remove corn from the water, drain thoroughly, and pat dry. Baste ears with chile lime butter.

Arrange corn on the grill. Cook, turning often and basting with extra chile lime butter, for about 20 minutes, or until the husks are lightly charred and the corn is done. Serve...*with plenty of napkins!*

Serves 3 to 6

Chile Paste

To make your own paste using dried chilies, start with any combination of dried ancho, chipotle, casabel, or other chilies. *(The heat of the paste will depend on the varieties of chilies you use.)* Remove the stems and seeds. Pour boiling water over the chilies to cover and soak for 30 minutes. Drain and thoroughly puree in a food processor. (You may need to press the paste through a sieve to produce a totally smooth paste.) The paste can be stored, covered and refrigerated, for about 2 weeks. Or, freeze small portions on a cookie sheet and transfer to a zippered freezer bag when firm.

Chile pastes are very popular throughout Southeast Asia and are used to add heat to a dish. The pastes can be added during cooking or can be used as a condiment on the table.

Frijoles Refritos

Translated, frijoles refritos means refried beans.

*Normally, refried beans have very little zip! These are without a doubt the **tastiest** I have tried!*

*Delicious topped with
shredded cheddar cheese, sour cream, and chopped red onion
or served plain as a side dish to any Mexican entrée.*

2 tablespoons sesame oil
1 cup diced onion
3 cloves garlic, minced
1-pound can black beans, drained
   (liquid reserved)

1-pound can pinto beans, drained
   (liquid reserved)
1 teaspoon cumin
1 teaspoon salt
1 teaspoon black pepper
Splash or two of hot sauce

Heat 2 tablespoons of oil over medium heat. Add onion and garlic. Sauté for about 10 minutes, stirring occasionally.

Add beans, spices, and hot sauce along with 1/2 cup of reserved bean liquid. Mash the beans. Continue to mash and cook until smooth and nearly pureed, adding more bean liquid if needed (about 8 minutes).

Serves 6

Roasted Mexican-Style Vegetables

*This combination of vegetables and spices
will make your taste buds dance with delight!
And the dish is so hearty, it could easily take center stage as a vegetarian entrée!*

1 medium onion, thinly sliced
1 medium red bell pepper (seeds removed),
   cut into 2" pieces)
1 medium yellow or orange bell pepper
   (seeds removed), cut into 2" pieces
2 large carrots, peeled and sliced 1/4" thick
1/4 medium red cabbage, cut into 2" pieces
2 medium Hungarian wax chile peppers
   (seeds and ribs removed), cut into very thin
   strips

1 cup canned kidney beans, drained
1 cup canned black beans, drained
1/4 cup corn oil
1/4 cup dry red wine
1/2 teaspoon cumin powder
2 teaspoons oregano flakes
1/8 teaspoon cayenne pepper
Sea salt to taste (1/2 to 1 teaspoon)

Combine first 8 ingredients in a large bowl.

In a separate (small) bowl, combine remaining 6 ingredients. Add to vegetables and stir well to blend.

Transfer to a baking sheet and roast in a 450-degree oven (no need to preheat oven) for about 50 minutes. Turn vegetables with a spatula several times during the last 20 minutes of roasting.

Serves 6

Sesame Green Beans

Green beans with an incredible, tantalizing Far Eastern flavour.

1 pound fresh string beans (tips removed)
2 tablespoons sesame oil
2 tablespoons finely sliced scallions (with green tops)
2 cloves garlic, minced

1/2 teaspoon freshly grated ginger
1 teaspoon reduced-sodium soy sauce
1/2 teaspoon hot sauce
1/8 teaspoon freshly ground black pepper

Pour about 1 cup of water into a steamer pan. Place green beans into the steamer basket, cover, and bring to a boil. Reduce heat to simmer and cook for 2 minutes. *(Don't overcook...beans should be bright green and slightly crisp.)* Rinse in a colander under cold water to stop further cooking. Set aside.

In a medium skillet, over moderate heat, combine sesame oil, scallions, garlic, and ginger. Sauté until scallions are soft.

Meanwhile, in a small dish, combine soy sauce with hot sauce and black pepper. Add to skillet and stir.

Stir in steamed green beans and heat through.

Serves 4

Red Rice

.

There are many variations of Red Rice.
I like to modify the basic recipe by adding vegetables I happen to have on hand.
Fresh corn, sweet green peas, chopped carrots, and celery always add a nice touch.
I have also added chopped ham or crispy crumbled bacon.
The basic recipe below is a great starting point for adding your own creative touch!

1 cup uncooked rice
2 cups hot water
3 tablespoons bacon drippings
1 cup chicken broth
8 ounce can tomato sauce
5 whole scallions with green tops (chopped)

1 clove garlic, minced
Salt to taste
1 tablespoon Chili Powder (24)
1/2 teaspoon cumin
Pinch of crushed dried oregano

Pour hot water over rice and let it stand for about 15 minutes. Drain the rice and shake in a strainer to remove any excess water.

In a heavy skillet, brown rice in bacon drippings over low heat.

Add remaining ingredients and bring to a boil. Cover, reduce heat, and cook for 20 to 25 minutes.

Stir with a fork, transfer to a bowl, and serve!

Serves 4

Spanish Rice

If you have ever dined at a Mexican restaurant,
you likely noticed that Spanish Rice is served with every entrée.
Even though it's a little spicy,
it has the tendency to calm the palette in the event of a fiery occurrence
from an accompanying dish!

4-1/2 cups cooked white rice
1/2 cup Spanish olive oil
1 large white onion, chopped
1 cup chopped green bell pepper
1/4 cup finely chopped fresh cilantro
1/4 cup tomato paste

1 cup water
1 teaspoon salt
1/8 teaspoon pepper
2 teaspoons Chili Powder (24)
1/8 teaspoon cayenne pepper

While rice is cooking, place oil, onion, green pepper, and cilantro in a large frying pan and sauté until onion is lightly browned.

In a small bowl, combine tomato paste with water and stir until smooth. Stir in seasonings. Add to onion and pepper mixture. Bring to a boil. Simmer for about 5 minutes.

Add cooked rice, stir, and continue cooking over low to medium heat for about 5 minutes, or until flavours are blended through.

Serves 8

Happy Endings to Tame the Flame

- ❑ *Apple Enchilladas*

- ❑ *Caramel Flan*

- ❑ *Fried Ice Cream*

- ❑ *Fried Milk*

- ❑ *Lemon Flan*

- ❑ *Mexican Wedding Cakes*

- ❑ *Peach Fajitas Al-a-Mode*

- ❑ *Pumpkin Empanadas*

- ❑ *Sopaipillas*

Apple Enchiladas

Apples rolled in flour tortillas… very simple to make.

21-ounce can apple pie filling
6 8" flour tortillas
1/3 cup butter
1/2 cup sugar

1/2 cup brown sugar, packed
1 teaspoon ground cinnamon
1/2 cup water
Cinnamon sugar *(for sprinkling)*

Preheat oven to 350 degrees. Lightly grease a 9 x 11" baking pan.

Spoon equal parts of apple filling onto tortillas and spread to edges.

Roll tortillas and place in prepared baking pan, seam-side-down.

In a medium saucepan, bring butter, sugars, cinnamon, and water to a boil. Reduce heat and simmer, stirring constantly for 3 minutes.

Pour sauce evenly over tortillas. Sprinkle lightly with cinnamon sugar.

Bake for 20 minutes.

Serve as is or with whipped cream or ice cream.

Serves 6

Caramel Flan

This creamy custard with caramel sauce presents an elegant ending to any fine meal.

1/2 cup sugar	2/3 cup sugar
3 whole eggs	3 cups whole milk
3 egg yolks	2 teaspoons vanilla extract

Preheat oven to 350 degrees. Butter a 9" flan pan.

In a skillet over medium heat, cook 1/2 cup of sugar, stirring constantly, until it is melted and turns dark brown (about 5 minutes). *(Use extreme caution! Cooked sugar is very hot and can burn the skin if it spatters!)*

Immediately pour the hot caramel syrup into the baking pan and swirl the pan until the bottom is coated. *(The caramel will harden at this point and melt again later as the flan bakes.)*

In a large mixing bowl, gently but thoroughly whisk eggs, egg yolks, and 2/3 cup of sugar. Gradually add milk, whisking after each addition. Stir in vanilla.

Pour the custard mixture into the prepared pan. Set the flan in a larger baking pan that has been filled about 1/4 full with boiling water. *(The water should come no more than halfway up the sides of the flan pan.)*

Bake until a knife inserted two-thirds of the way to the center comes out clean (about 35 to 40 minutes). *(The center should still be slightly soft, as the flan will finish cooking after it is removed from the oven.)* Cool in the water bath, then remove the baking pan from the bath and refrigerate for about 2 hours.

Before serving, run a sharp knife around the edge of the flan to release it. Place a large, rimmed serving plate over the baking pan. Using both hands, invert both so that the flan and the liquid sauce release onto the plate. Refrigerate until serving time.

Serves 8

Fried Ice Cream

What a fun way to celebrate dessert!

*This delicious Mexican favorite is crunchy and warm on the outside,
cold, creamy, and refreshing on the inside.*

1 pint good-quality vanilla ice cream
1/2 cup crushed corn flake crumbs
1 teaspoon ground cinnamon
2 teaspoons sugar

1 egg
Oil for deep frying
Honey *(or chocolate sauce or hot fudge!)*
Whipped cream

Scoop out 4 balls of ice cream. Put in a small pan and return to freezer.

Mix corn flake crumbs, cinnamon, and sugar in a small bowl. Roll frozen ice cream balls in half the crumb mixture until coated. Return to freezer.

Beat egg. Dip coated ice cream balls in egg and roll again in remaining crumbs. Freeze until ready to use.

When ready to serve, heat oil to 350 degrees. Place 1 frozen ice cream ball in fryer basket or on a perforated spoon and lower into hot oil for one 1 minute. Immediately remove, drain, and place in a dessert dish. Drizzle with honey or chocolate and top with a dollop of whipped cream. *(While doing this, the oil will come back to temperature for the remaining ice cream balls.)* Repeat with each of the three remaining balls.

Serves 4

Fried Milk

A creamy custard interior… wrapped in a golden, crunchy, and delicious crust!

*'Snaz it up a little with some white chocolate sauce, whipped cream, and a cherry…
or just serve alone.*

1/2 cup sugar
1/2 cup cornstarch
1/4 teaspoon freshly grated nutmeg
3 cups milk
1 tablespoon butter

1/4 teaspoon grated lemon zest
2 eggs, beaten
3/4 cup dry bread crumbs
About 1/4 cup vegetable oil
Confectioners' sugar

Mix sugar, cornstarch, and nutmeg in a saucepan. Gradually stir in milk. Bring to a boil over medium heat, stirring constantly. Reduce heat and cook for one minute, stirring constantly.

Remove from heat. Stir in butter and lemon zest.

Spread mixture in a buttered 8 x 8" pan. Cool and then refrigerate, uncovered, for at least 3 hours.

Cut into 2" squares. Dip squares into egg and coat with breadcrumbs.

In a large skillet, fry squares in oil until light brown on one sided. Turn and continue frying until the opposite side is also lightly browned. Remove from pan and drain on paper towels. Place on a platter and sprinkle with confectioners' sugar.

Serve while still warm. If any is left, refrigerate and eat cold!

Serves 12

Lemon Flan

*This simple-to-prepare dessert makes a light but exquisite ending to your meal.
For even greater efficiency, make it a day ahead and refrigerate.*

2 cups nonfat milk

2 cups sugar

2 tablespoons grated lemon zest

1/2 cup flour

8 eggs

4 tablespoons melted butter

1 tablespoon raw sugar crystals

Butter a 9" flan pan and preheat oven to 350 degrees.

Whirl first six ingredients in a blender for 2 or 3 minutes. Pour into prepared pan. Bake for 40 to 45 minutes or until center tests done. Sprinkle raw sugar on top and place under the broiler until lightly browned.

Serve warm or cold.

Serves 6 to 8

Mexican Wedding Cakes

These little cookies are actually not cakes at all!...(Surprise !!!)

1 cup butter, room temperature
1-1/2 cup confectioners' sugar (divided)
1/4 teaspoon salt

1 teaspoon vanilla extract
2 cups sifted flour

Preheat oven to 400 degrees.

Cream butter. Add 1/2 cup confectioners' sugar and blend in. Stir in salt, vanilla, and flour until dough forms a ball. Chill for several hours.

Scoop up small pieces of dough, roll with hands to form balls almost the size of a golf ball.

Place on ungreased cookie sheets and bake for about 12 minutes or until golden.

While the cookies are still hot, roll in remaining 1 cup of confectioners' sugar. Place on a wire rack to cool.

Makes 24

Peach Fajitas Al-a-Mode

A great way to end a Mexican fiesta.

4 cups peaches, peeled and sliced	1 teaspoon cinnamon
1/2 cup brown sugar	1/4 cup sugar
1/4 cup instant tapioca	4 tablespoons butter
1 cup dry white wine	4 6" flour tortillas
1/3 teaspoon cinnamon	Ice cream *(vanilla or peach)*
1/4 teaspoon cayenne pepper	Chopped pecans

Put first six ingredients into a saucepan, stir, and let stand. After 30 minutes, cook over medium heat, stirring until mixture reaches a full boil and the tapioca is soft. Set aside.

Make a mixture with 1 teaspoon of cinnamon and 1/4 cup sugar.

Melt 1 tablespoon of butter in a large skillet. Add a tortilla and sauté for 30 seconds. Lightly sprinkle with some cinnamon sugar. Turn. Sauté an additional 30 seconds. Sprinkle again. Transfer to a serving plate. Repeat with remaining tortillas.

Spread a fourth of the peach mixture over half of each tortilla and fold.

Serve with ice cream. Sprinkle with pecans.

Serves 4

Pumpkin Empanadas

These great little gems make a terrific dessert!
Try serving warm with ice cream.

1-1/4 cups pumpkin puree
3/4 cup granulated sugar
1/4 teaspoon ground nutmeg
1/4 teaspoon ground cinnamon
1/4 teaspoon ground ginger
4 cups all-purpose flour
1/2 cup sugar
1 tablespoon plus 1 teaspoon baking powder

1 teaspoon salt
1-1/3 cups shortening
1 cup plus 2 tablespoons cold whole milk
  (divided)
1 egg yolk, beaten
1/4 cup sugar
1/2 teaspoon ground cinnamon

Combine pumpkin, 3/4 cup of sugar, nutmeg, cinnamon, and ginger. Stir well and refrigerate.

In a separate bowl, combine flour, 1/2 cup of sugar, baking powder, and salt. Cut in shortening with a pastry blender until mixture resembles coarse crumbs. Sprinkle 1 cup of milk evenly over flour mixture and stir lightly with a fork until all dry ingredients are moistened. Shape into a ball and chill for about 2 hours.

Preheat oven to 450 degrees.

Roll chilled dough to 1/8" thickness and cut into 4" circles. Place a heaping tablespoon of pumpkin mixture in the center of each circle. Moisten edges with additional milk. Fold circles in half, and press edges together with a fork.

Brush empanadas with egg yolk and place on ungreased baking sheets. Pierce tops of empanadas to vent. Bake for 8 minutes. Transfer baking sheet to 6" from broiler. Broil *(watching carefully!)* until golden.

Combine 1/4 cup of sugar with 1/2 teaspoon of cinnamon.

When empanadas are done, remove from oven and transfer to a wire rack. Sprinkle with cinnamon sugar. Serve warm or cold.

Makes 2 Dozen

Sopaipillas

Pronounced "SO pa PEE yas"...
This is a delicious puff pastry dessert that is sometimes served drizzled with honey.
Sopaipillas can also be served with soups or stews in place of bread.

2 cups all-purpose flour
1 teaspoon baking powder
1 teaspoon salt
2 tablespoons solid vegetable shortening
(About) 3/4 cup warm water
Vegetable oil for deep frying

1 cup heavy cream
1 teaspoon sugar
1/2 teaspoon pure vanilla extract
1/2 cup honey
Cinnamon

Sift the dry ingredients into a bowl. Using your fingers, rub the shortening into the flour mixture until it resembles fine breadcrumbs. Gradually add just enough water until the dough begins to form. Wrap the dough in plastic wrap and allow it to rest for one hour.

Working with half of the dough at a time, roll out into a square, keeping it as even and thin as possible. (You may need a little extra flour to prevent sticking.) Cut the dough into 3" squares. Repeat with the second piece of dough.

Pour oil into a large, heavy pot. Heat to 375 degrees.

Add a few pastry squares at a time and use tongs to push the pastry down into the oil. Cook until golden brown on both sides, turning once. Remove sopaipillas from the oil and place on paper towels to drain.

Whip cream with 1 teaspoon of sugar until it forms soft peaks. Stir in vanilla.

Drizzle sopaipillas with honey and sprinkle with cinnamon. Serve with whipped cream.

Index (To Find Hot Stuff!)

A

B

C

M

N

P

Q

R

Adios, mis amigos!...y recuerde...¡El Calor está En, el Bebé!

*(Adios, my friends...and remember...**The Heat's On, Baby!**)*